Divine Disclosure

*Also by D.S. Russell
and published by Fortress Press*

Between the Testaments

DIVINE DISCLOSURE

An Introduction to Jewish Apocalyptic

D.S. Russell

FORTRESS PRESS   MINNEAPOLIS

Copyright © D.S. Russell 1992

ISBN 0-8006-2698

LCCN 92-9523

Library of Congress
Cataloging-in-Publication data available.

Phototypeset by Intype, London
and printed in Great Britain by
Mackays of Chatham, Kent

Contents

Preface

The subject of Jewish apocalyptic was complicated enough when I first ventured into print on the subject more than thirty years ago. Since then it has grown, not only in importance, but also in complexity so that it has become increasingly difficult, for the general reader at any rate, to 'see the wood for the trees'.

For some time I have felt the need for a short, but fairly comprehensive, Introduction which, hopefully, might help towards a better understanding of the subject without entering into too many technical details. This short Introduction is offered with that aim in view. Much more could have been written and more detail supplied, but that might well have undermined the aim of the book to keep the treatment as uncomplicated as possible. Some of the ground covered here I have already covered in other writings; but I have taken the opportunity to indicate where my judgments have changed and have attempted to explain the reasons why.

The immediate occasion for the writing of the book was an invitation received from McMaster Divinity College in Canada to deliver a series of lectures on Jewish apocalyptic to a group of 'mature' lay students whose knowledge of the subject was minimal. I am most grateful to the Principal and to the other members of staff, as well as to the student body, for the opportunity thus given and for the warmth of their reception. The lectures given on that occasion have been rewritten in the hope that they will be found helpful to a wider readership.

My indebtedness to many scholars will be obvious throughout the book, an indebtedness which, I trust, I have properly acknowledged.

The subject is an important one, not only for an understanding of 'intertestamental' Judaism, but also for the origins of Christianity; besides this, I believe it has a worthwhile message for our own day and generation.

I offer this book in gratitude for all that I myself have received, and trust it will be a help to at least some.

D.S. Russell

Bristol

Introduction

I. THE RE-BIRTH OF APOCALYPTIC STUDY

The subject of Jewish apocalyptic is not everyone's idea of 'a good read'! To the newcomer this style of writing is, to say the least, both confused and confusing. It seems to belong to 'the Old Testament tradition', and yet it is distinctly different from it. Its origins are obscure, its style is strange and its subject-matter seems to raise more problems than it solves. Its prognostications, moreover, have for centuries been the happy-hunting-ground of fundamentalist Christian sects and have had a peculiar fascination for cranks and charlatans with their charts of aeons and dispensations into which history is believed to be divided as a prelude to 'the End', who speak excitedly of 'the Rapture', who point to the awful battle of Armageddon as a necessary prelude to the Second Coming of Christ, who discuss theological truth in terms of 'pre-millennialism' and 'post-millennialism' and point to the catastrophic and devastating end of the world at a precise date and in precise circumstances foretold in scripture.

It would be a thousand pities, however, if such literature were to be dismissed out of hand as something 'alien' either to the Jewish tradition or to the Christian gospel. As we shall see, the apocalyptic literature deserves an honoured place within Judaism and did much to shape the conceptual world of the first Christian century and, as a result, deeply influenced the faith and expectations of the early Christian church, not least in its eschatological and messianic beliefs. It is not too strong to say that early Christianity was deeply indebted to the apocalyptic tradition which, despite all the dangers associated with its abuse, made possible the development of an originally Jewish sect into a world religion with a universal and indeed cosmic dimension to its message which it otherwise might not have had. The Book of Revelation is the outstanding New Testament example of this style of writing. But it would be wrong to single out this book from all the rest as if it were simply a rather odd appendage to the New Testament which sits uneasily with the Gospels and epistles. The fact is that the concepts and thought-forms so common in Jewish apocalyptic provide much of the background to both Gospels and epistles. There is no saying what Christianity would have been like if it had not entered into such a world with its peculiarly apocalyptic eschatological hopes and expectations. No doubt, by the mercy of God, it would have survived and have grown and flourished. But its resulting form and expression would surely have been quite different from what they turned out to be (see the final chapter).

This being so, the study of Jewish apocalyptic is of considerable importance if we are to understand the origins and development of the Christian faith and is of much more than merely antiquarian interest where the development of the Jewish religion itself is concerned. Judaism chose to follow a different path and, in course of time, eschewed apocalyptic, although its influence did not altogether disappear but continued to make its presence felt right on into the Christian era. It is good to know that serious attempts are now being made by Jewish and Christian scholars alike to 'rescue' apocalyptic from the precarious position it has for long held and to re-establish it, not as something that has been discredited, but rather as a rich vein to be mined for the better understanding of both Judaism and Christianity.

During the first half of this present century students of the subject had to rely heavily on writers like R. H. Charles in English and Kautzsch, Volz and Bousset in German for a knowledge of the relevant texts. For the English reader Charles' two large volumes entitled *The Apocrypha and Pseudepigrapha of the Old Testament*, published in 1913, provided the 'staple diet'.[1] The publication of a small book by H.H. Rowley in 1944, subsequently revised and enlarged, came as a welcome addition to the available literature on the subject – *The Relevance of*

Apocalyptic.[2] Up to the time of that publication relatively little interest had been taken in the apocalyptic literature generally by Old Testament scholars, in Britain at any rate, despite the efforts of R.H. Charles and others. It is of interest in this connection to observe with E.W. Nicholson[3] that in all the weighty volumes published by the Society for Old Testament Studies highlighting the various aspects of Old Testament study deserving of careful examination, not until 1979 did the subject of apocalyptic win more than passing reference. In *The People and the Book*, edited by A.S. Peake and published in 1925, only a few incidental references are made to the subject. In *Record and Revelation*, edited by H. Wheeler Robinson and published in 1938, it gains only passing reference in a chapter on the literature of Israel; and in *The Old Testament and Modern Study*, edited by H.H. Rowley and published in 1951, it is barely mentioned at all. Not until 1979, in *Tradition and Interpretation*, edited by G.W. Anderson, was it given prominence, an entire chapter being devoted to it from the pen of E.W. Nicholson. His article indicates clearly that between 1951 and 1979 there had grown up a most lively interest in apocalyptic – an interest that has continued to grow and has spread fruitfully into other fields of study besides that of the Old Testament itself, bringing fresh light to bear on early Judaism and its relation to the hellenistic culture, on the study of Christian origins, and on New Testament study and Christian theology generally. Since then there has been a veritable spate of literature relating to apocalyptic – Christian as well as Jewish – which shows little sign of abating.

There is in the apocalyptic literature a great deal of dross that can readily be discarded, but there is gold to be found there too if only we will have the patience and the vision to discover what and where it is. In this small Introduction an attempt will be made to bring up to date some of the tentative findings of scholarly research in this field in the hope that the reader will find something here and there that will make the search for better understanding worthwhile.

2. REASONS FOR THIS RE-BIRTH OF INTEREST

(a) Availability of new texts

Present-day readers have an advantage over those of a generation or so ago on at least two counts. One is that many texts have been discovered in the intervening years, a number of them of an apocalyptic kind. The other is that both these and the texts already known are now available in good English translation, sometimes with helpful commentaries. There are, for example, the two large volumes on *The Old Testament Pseudepigrapha* edited by James H. Charlesworth, published in 1983 and 1985,[4] the first of which gives a rich array of apocalyptic and testamentary works, and the volume edited by H.F.D. Sparks entitled *The Apocryphal Old Testament*, published in 1984.[5]

The most dramatic documents, discovered in the 1940s, were the Scrolls found at Qumran near the shores of the Dead Sea. These Scrolls and others from adjacent sites were the work or the property of a company of Jews who have been described as 'a hotted up apocalyptic sect'. Whether that is an apt title or not, a fairly large number of documents and fragments were found there representing known apocalyptic books including the canonical Book of Daniel in which they were obviously greatly interested, together with a number of others which were their own production and which demonstrate those same apocalyptic characteristics and emphases which are familiar to us from elsewhere. We shall look further at some of these writings in our next chapter.

Alongside these, though of a different date and of a different kind, are the Nag Hammadi texts from Egypt which reflect a form of Gnosticism akin in many ways to that of Jewish apocalyptic, demonstrating a pessimism with regard to all earthly structures and a consequent escape into other-worldly speculation.

(b) Recognition of its importance for theological study

But alongside the discoveries of new texts and their greater availability has gone a greater awareness of their significance for Christian theology generally and systematic theology in particular. Such a change is all the more noteworthy when we recall that a previous generation of scholars had tended to denigrate apocalyptic almost altogether, relegating it to the sidelines or else treating it as if it were an embarrassment to biblical scholarship. G. F. Moore, for example, in his great work on Judaism[6] minimizes the indebtedness of Judaism (and so of Christianity) to apocalyptic and argues that since these books were never recognized by Judaism in the way that the rabbinic tradition, for example, was, it is wrong to see in them a primary source or, in his words, 'to contaminate its theology with them'. They had nothing to contribute to what he describes as 'normative Judaism' to be found in the teachers of the rabbinic line. This same contention is supported by a scholar such as R.T. Herford[7] who goes further than Moore in describing apocalyptic as a dangerous influence, the product of weak minds and unbalanced judgments, the work of men driven to the very edge of distraction, and concludes that Judaism 'owed nothing of its strength and depth to apocalyptic teaching'.

It can hardly be denied that there is much in this literature that is both otiose and irrelevant. Nevertheless, there is much too that is informative and of lasting worth. It is now affirmed by an increasing number of scholars that apocalyptic indeed represents a significant development within the Judaism of the intertestamental period and is an important factor in understanding not only the historical background of the New Testament, but also its theological appreciation. It helps to bridge the gap between the Old Testament and the New, illuminating as no other source can do certain significant developments in religious belief that emerged during the intertestamental years, especially those of an eschatological and messianic kind. Besides this, as we shall see later, it has a message which, if re-interpreted in terms of our own contemporary and cultural pattern, has something powerful to say to us at this present time.

Klaus Koch, in his important book *The Rediscovery of Apocalyptic*[8] refers in this connection to two seminal writers among German-speaking scholars who have demonstrated the importance of apocalyptic for an understanding of Christian theology. The first is Ernst Käsemann in his essay entitled 'The Beginnings of Christian Theology' published in 1960 in which he sums up his conclusions in a single sentence which has led to much debate and controversy: 'Apocalyptic was the mother of all Christian theology'.[9] 'Up to then' writes Koch, 'apocalyptic had been for biblical scholars something on the periphery of the Old and New Testaments – something bordering on heresy. Käsemann had suddenly declared that a tributary was the main stream from which everything else at the end of the Old Testament and the beginning of the New was allegedly fed'.[10] Arguments will no doubt continue about Käsemann's claim; but this at least can be said that the study of Jewish apocalyptic is of no small importance for an understanding not only of late Old Testament prophecy but also of the Gospels and epistles of the New Testament.[11]

But the importance of apocalyptic has been increasingly recognized, not only by biblical and New Testament theologians, but also by systematic theologians. And this brings us to the second name mentioned by Koch. In 1959 Wolfhart Pannenberg, in his essay entitled 'Redemptive Event and History',[12] gave renewed importance to the apocalyptic concept of history for Christian theology. In apocalyptic the concept of universal history was developed and became an important factor in Christian belief. Further impetus has come from the writings of Jürgen Moltmann[13] who, in the words of P.D. Hanson, 'sees in the universal and cosmic perspective of apocalyptic an important safeguard against the snares of ethno-centricism and existentialistic narrowing of human history'.[14]

The apocalyptists were not, of course, systematic theologians; they were not interested in exact definitions of faith – and logic was one of their lesser virtues! Rather, they were visionaries and poets who expressed their convictions in terms of ancient and contemporary imagery, highly imaginative and often obscure. They were constantly inconsistent within their own writings and over against the writings of others of like mind. They tried to explain the inexplicable, to express in mere words the inexpressible mysteries of God. Inconsistency in such circumstances can perhaps be excused as a minor sin! But, despite this, their influence on their generation was quite considerable and the contribution they were able to make to religious thought has been increasingly recognized, as has been said, in our own generation.

To sum up, then: what we have seen in the past fifty years or so has been a significant development in the place given to apocalyptic thought in the history of biblical and theological interpretation about which much controversy continues. Having been regarded, in its biblical expression at any rate, as the happy-hunting-ground of fundamentalist sects, and having been looked down upon by academic theology or simply by-passed as beneath serious consideration, the apocalyptic literature has come to assume a significant role in serious biblical and theological debate.

(c) Its affinity with today's world

But there is a third reason which helps to explain the re-discovery and revival of interest in apocalyptic in recent times – a marked affinity between the events of the intertestamental period and those of this present generation, an affinity that engenders both empathy and understanding.

In 1975 James Barr wrote an article entitled 'Jewish apocalyptic in recent scholarly study'[15] in which he criticized H.H. Rowley's attempt to show the relevance of apocalyptic to our own age which, in Barr's judgment, is 'basically non-apocalyptic in its attitudes and sympathies'. It is perfectly true, of course, that there is much in the language and teaching of the apocalyptists which is altogether foreign to our modern way of thinking – its descriptive journeys into the heavenly world, its fantastic imagery, its proliferation of angels, its confrontation of cosmic and celestial armies, its predetermination of historical events, its speculations concerning human destiny and so forth. To this extent ours can indeed be said to be a 'non-apocalyptic' age. And yet, despite this disparity, there is a marked similarity, not least in historical background and expectation between that generation and ours that makes such literature less alien and less irrelevant than it otherwise might have been. We recall, for example, that Jewish apocalypses like the Book of Daniel arose in times of severe crisis and, in some cases, in response to the experience of suffering and persecution and the ravages of war. We shall see in the second chapter how true this was of the author of Daniel, faced as he was with the tyranny of the Seleucid king, Antiochus IV Epiphanes. Not all the apocalyptic writings were the direct outcome of such conditions, but together they reflect the belief that the time was speedily coming when the forces of good would be confronted by the forces of evil. There would be the greatest show-down the world had ever seen in which the very cosmos itself would become embroiled. The powers of darkness would be destroyed and the sons of light would receive victory at the hands of God.

Given the terrifying political and military scenario of the late twentieth century, it is perhaps hardly suprising that many have seen in the events of our modern world a reflection of those intertestamental days as described in the words and imagery of the apocalyptic literature. Commenting on the disdainful attitude adopted by many in the nineteenth century towards apocalyptic with its message of 'doom and gloom', P.D. Hanson asserts that, with the coming of the twentieth century, the mood suddenly began to change:

In the aftermath of the First World War an answer began to take shape to the question, why read a literature interpreting reality in terms of conflict and tension and replete with bizarre symbols and mythical figures? The answer arose among inhabitants of a ravaged and broken planet, to whom apocalyptic literature seemed more accurately to describe reality as it actually was experienced than did the constructions of the philosophical idealists and the harmonious systems of the theological liberals. For Karl Barth in World War I and Hans Lilje in World War II the Book of Revelation was far from absurd, being instead a profoundly truthful portrait of the forces contending for control of the world.[16]

On the more 'popular' level too, words like 'apocalypse' and 'apocalyptic' are fairly commonplace among us today. 'Apocalypse' is the subject of novels, plays, films and even computer games, providing a back-drop of indescribable horror and bloodshed. It sums up all that we mean when we speak of absolute catastrophe and the total collapse of society. It refers to the utter havoc wrought by nuclear warfare and points to the obliteration of the human race and the devastation of the earth. It conjures up in our minds a cataclysmic end to life itself on this planet.

It takes particularly graphic shape in the form of science-fiction with its inter-galactic wars against aliens from outer space or from worlds other than our own in which the whole human species is placed in dire peril. The picture becomes all the more graphic when fiction becomes fact as has happened more than once in wars of recent times with their acclaimed forces of good arrayed against the forces of evil, the fire-scorched earth, the earth-shattering eruptions of high explosive bombs and so on. It is small wonder that, for this reason alone, this generation has recognized a certain affinity with the graphic language of this ancient literature. Apocalyptic in its modern and popular usage may be far removed from what these ancient writers meant by the word: nevertheless the star wars scenario and its expression in modern warfare provides a graphic setting within which some at least of the fearful significance of these apocalyptic texts can be more readily understood.

It is not surprising that, in the words of P.D. Hanson, 'a modern world, slipping into a deeper and deeper pessimism regarding the future, has turned to the literature of an ancient era similarly plagued by pessimism vis-a-vis human possibilities'.[17] He rightly speaks of the 'pessimism' expressed in these writings; but he is wise to qualify this by adding the words 'vis-a-vis human possibilities', for, as we shall see later, though pessimistic about their own ability to save themselves, the apocalyptists were sustained by a buoyant faith that enabled them to overcome.

That same faith, so often demonstrated in times of crisis and persecution, has prevailed in generation after generation and is to be found not least in our own. It has continued to find nourishment in this form of literature which, for all its strangeness, provides an unfailing source of strength to people in dire need. Many, it is true, have found in it an escape from the hard realities of life; but some have found in it a strength for daily living. As I have said elsewhere, 'apocalyptic . . . lifts up its voice to give needed reassurance to God's people . . . Like an underground stream it has flowed on undetected, sometimes for centuries at a time, breaking surface every now and again, particularly in times of crisis and persecution, to bring refreshment and strength to the harassed people of God. The hopes and fears expressed in the apocalyptic writings are always there just below the surface of religious thought and experience. They may find new expression and renewed interpretation, but their essential message has a relevance in every age of crisis, not least our own.'[18]

I

The Literature: Identification and Definition

1. BOOKS AND MORE BOOKS

The period with which this book is concerned extends from the time of Alexander the Great (356–323 BC) to the second century of the Christian era, and more particularly the years 250 BC to AD 100.[1]

(a) A spate of books

During that time, throughout the hellenistic world, a veritable spate of books appeared to which allusion is made in Eccles 12.12: 'Of the making of books there is no end, and much study is a weariness of the flesh.' No doubt the writer had in mind the voluminous literary output of the Greek world towards the end of the third century BC; but his words might have applied equally well to the Jewish literature that flowed from many a pen in the centuries that followed. Some of these works are known to us only by their titles or by brief references or quotations in other literature. Those that have survived are of a diverse kind, ranging from history to legend, from philosophy to fiction, from poetry to propaganda tracts.

We are not concerned here with the growth of the 'canonical' scriptures which took place during this time or with the emergence of the Greek translation of the Hebrew scriptures, known as the Septuagint (LXX), except in so far as these have a direct bearing on the apocalyptic writings which are our particular concern here. We simply note at this point that a number of extra-canonical books written in Palestine in Hebrew or Aramaic, some of them of an

I

apocalyptic kind, were also later translated into Greek and became popular with Greek-speaking Jews in the Dispersion. In course of time certain of these came to be incorporated in the Septuagint which was subsequently taken over by the Christian church.

(b) The 'outside books': Apocrypha and pseudepigrapha

The word used at a subsequent date by the rabbis to describe those extra-canonical books, whether incorporated in the Septuagint or not, was *hisonim* meaning 'external' or 'outside (books)'. The word 'apocryphal' came to have the same designation, namely those books that lie outside the canon. In more recent times, however, it has acquired a more restricted use, signifying those books that found their way into the Greek and Latin manuscripts of the scripture (i.e. the Septuagint and the Vulgate) as distinct from those that did not. The former was known as 'Apocrypha' among Protestants and 'Deutero-canonical' among Roman Catholics; the latter, together with others subsequently written, are described as 'pseudepigrapha' among Protestants and 'apocryphal writings' among Roman Catholics. There is no agreed list of these pseudepigraphal/apocryphal writings, nor indeed is there complete agreement concerning the contents of the Apocrypha itself.

The word 'pseudepigrapha' is a transliteration of a Greek word meaning 'with false subscription', referring to books written under an assumed name. But it is misleading for at least two good reasons: there are, first, non-pseudepigraphal books among those thus classified and, secondly, there are pseudepigraphal books outside this classifiction!

There is indeed no agreed list of such writings, as has been said, if only because there are no agreed criteria by which they should be determined. Elsewhere I have tried to draw up such criteria in these words:

Generally speaking, the expression 'pseudepigrapha', in its early Jewish context, may be said to refer to a body of diverse writings in the Jewish or Jewish-Christian traditions which (a) are not included in the Old or New Testaments, the Apocrypha and the rabbinic literature, (b) are associated with the biblical books or biblical characters, (c) are more often than not written in the name of some ancient biblical worthy, (d) convey a message from God that is relevant to the time at which the books were written and

(e) are written during the period 200 BC–AD 200 or, if later than this, preserve Jewish traditions of that same period.[2]

The measure of disagreement among scholars as to what are and what are not to be counted among the pseudepigrapha can be gauged by an examination of the different lists of books presented under this heading.[3]

(c) Types of literature

The types of literature represented among the 'outside books' are very varied. A significant number are in the form of *testaments* in which the speaker is often a patriarch or other ancient worthy, addressing his sons as he contemplates his own death. The form they take is fairly uniform and the contents follow a recognizable pattern. Ethical exhortations are normally placed within a historical perspective and are followed by an eschatological prediction made known to the speaker by divine revelation. Some of these testaments are embedded in apocalypses, whilst others contain apocalyptic sections or elements. Perhaps the best known of such writings is the Testaments of the XII Patriarchs which seems to be rather heavily interpolated with Christian comment and is probably a redaction of a Jewish work of the second century BC. (For a list of such testamentary books see p. 7.)

A second category is the *midrash-type* writing in which the writer embellishes the text of scripture with his own observations and allusions, often going well beyond the evidence of scripture itself. The best known pseudepigraphon of this kind is the Book of Jubilees, also called 'the Little Genesis', being based on Genesis and part of Exodus and taking the form of a revelation given by God to Moses on Mount Sinai. Other writings of this type are the Letter of Aristeas, the Martyrdom of Isaiah, the Life of Adam and Eve, the Lives of the Prophets, Joseph and Asenath, *Liber Antiquitatum Biblicarum*, IV Baruch, Jannes and Jambres, Eldad and Modad and the Ladder of Jacob. A particularly interesting writing of this type from Qumran is the Genesis Apocryphon which, like Jubilees, embellishes in a colourful way the biblical text.

A third category is that of *wisdom-literature* which makes use of folklore and indulges in philosophical comment as in the Story of Ahikar,

III Maccabees, IV Maccabees, Pseudo-Phocylides and Syrian Menander.

A fourth type expresses itself in the form of *hymns and prayers* as in the Psalms of Solomon, the Prayer of Manasseh, Five Apocryphal Syriac Psalms, the Prayer of Joseph and the Prayer of Jacob.

A fifth category, which is our particular concern here, is that of *apocalyptic* where, as we shall see, the writer speaks in the name of some revered man of the past (as also in the *testaments*) recording certain hidden things concerning the cosmos and the end of the age which have been disclosed to him by divine relevation (For a list of such apocalyptic books see p. 7.)

(d) The Dead Sea Scrolls

The writings just mentioned, plentiful though they are, are only part of a larger literature produced during the intertestamental years among which are the celebrated Scrolls discovered in the caves of Qumran and neighbouring sites near the shores of the Dead Sea. The chief value of these Scrolls for a study of the intertestamental period is to be found in the contribution they make to our understanding of that complex Judaism which flourished at the beginning of the Christian era and which contained many splinter groups some of whose names have long since disappeared. Matthew Black describes the situation as 'one of widespread and dangerously proliferating and fissiparous heteropraxis, a kind of baptizing nonconformity, with many splinter groups extending from Judaea to Samaria and beyond into the Dispersion itself'.[4] A branch of the Essenes situated at Qumran was one such group, others of which, according to Philo and Josephus, were to be found in many villages and towns throughout Palestine as well as in separate communities away from the lawlessness of the cities.

It is a continuing matter of debate how many of these Scrolls, if any, should be counted in the classification 'pseudepigrapha'. More important for our purpose, however, is the question whether the Qumran community is representative of the apocalyptic movement and in particular whether the literature they themselves produced can rightly be designated by this name.

It is quite clear from an examination of the material found at

Qumran (both those documents already known to us and presumably originating elsewhere and that 'sectarian literature' peculiar to the community itself)[5] that there was indeed a close affinity between that community and other groups of apocalyptists from whom these known documents came. Such affinity is demonstrated, for example, by the fact that no fewer than seven different Qumran manuscripts of the Book of Daniel were found there, indicating its popularity among the members of the community. Other apocalyptic or apocalyptic-related books were also represented. The Book of Jubilees, for example, was well used, as indicated by the fact that fragments of at least ten manuscripts were found in the Qumran library. There is equally impressive evidence for the widespread use of I Enoch (in part) of which portions of ten Aramaic manuscripts were discovered. Besides these, fragments of sources believed to lie behind the Testaments of the XII Patriarchs have also been identified.

It is true that none of the 'sectarian literature' (documents actually produced by the community itself) takes the form of an apocalypse and on this ground it has been argued that it is not accurate to describe the sect as an 'apocalyptic community'. We shall see presently, however, that the word can in fact legitimately be used to describe material to be found in different literary forms and is not to be confined to the apocalypse-form alone and so can quite properly be used in this context. We may think in this connection of a number of apocalyptic-style writings portions of which have been found at Qumran such as the Book of Mysteries, a Description of the New Jerusalem, an Angel Liturgy, the Genesis Apocryphon and the Prayer of Nabonidus which closely resembles the account given in Daniel 4 concerning Nebuchadnezzar's miraculous recovery from illness.[6]

J. J. Collins illustrates the point by reference to the Damascus Document (CD) which has a close affinity with the Book of Jubilees, but he could have done so equally well by reference to several other Qumran writings besides:

CD is certainly not an apocalypse. The sect whose history it reflects had found a new medium of revelation in the inspired exegesis of the Teacher (of Righteousness) and did not rely on visions or ascents (to heaven) in the name of an ancient seer. Yet it also has significant affinities with the apocalypses of the Maccabean era in its claim to special revelation, use of periodization (of history), dualism and eschatology.

He concludes that such affinities 'strongly support the opinion that the Dead Sea sect originated in the same general milieu as the apocalyptic movements'.[7] There are marked differences, in both form and content, between these writings from Qumran and the apocalypses already known to us, but the evidence available from the whole range of the Qumran texts confirms the belief that the people of the Scrolls belonged to a milieu that can properly be called 'apocalyptic'.

2. APOCALYPTIC AND APOCALYPTIC LITERATURE

(a) Derivation

The word 'apocalyptic' is derived from a Greek word signfying 'to uncover', 'to unveil', usually with reference to something that has been hidden but has now been revealed. But such derivation of itself cannot properly express the wide range of meaning conveyed by it or by the corresponding noun 'apocalypse'. This is in fact a technical expression which came to be used by the Christian church from the second century onwards to indicate a type of literature akin to the New Testament Apocalypse of John which then gave its name to this style of writing. By its very nature, then, 'apocalyptic' is a difficult word to define. Indeed, so imprecise is it in general theological use – particularly as a noun – that it has been suggested it might conveniently be dropped altogether. We shall examine this question of definition below, but shall continue to use the word despite the limitations and possible misunderstandings such usage may carry with it.

(b) Identification

When we use the expression 'apocalyptic literature' we refer to a style of revelatory writing produced in Jewish circles approximately between the years 250 BC and AD 100 and taken up and perpetuated by the Christian church. As we shall see, it includes not only that genre of literature identified as 'apocalypse', but other genres besides which belong to the same milieu. At first sight its style of expression

6

is not a little off-putting to the modern reader. In its pages we find ourselves in 'a weird and wonderful world of fantasy and dreams – beasts with sprouting horns, dragons spouting fire, falling stars, mysterious horsemen, mystical mountains, sacred rivers, devastating earthquakes, fearsome giants, demon progeny, monstrous births, portents in heaven and portents on earth. Its often frenzied and frenetic descriptions of coming woes sound like the product of over-heated minds.'[8]

Our particular concern here is with those apocalyptic writings belonging to the intertestamental period. What exactly were they? The apocalyptic style of writing is most clearly represented in scripture by the Books of Daniel and Revelation. In this connection H.H. Rowley comments: 'It is by no accident that the one has been incorporated in the canon of the Old Testament and the other in that of the New. For they stand out far above all those others that stand between.'[9]

But what are 'those others'? As with the pseudepigrapha in general, so with the apocalyptic writings in particular, there is no agreed list of such books. Those that have perhaps the greatest claim to be recognized as apocalypses are as follows:

I Enoch (Ethiopic Book of Enoch), 3rd century BC to 1st century AD.

II Enoch (Slavonic Book of Enoch), late 1st century AD.

Apocalypse of Zephaniah, 1st century BC to 1st century AD.

Apocalypse of Abraham, 1st to 2nd century AD.

II Esdras (=4 Ezra) 3–14, c. AD 100.

II Baruch (Syriac Apocalypse of Baruch), early 2nd century AD.

Besides these there are other Jewish writings of the period which, though not themselves apocalypses, are nevertheless closely related to them and belong to the same milieu and are to be included in the classification 'apocalyptic literature'. These are:

The Book of Jubilees (The Little Genesis), 2nd century BC.

Testaments of the XII Patriarchs, 2nd century BC.

Treatise of Shem, 1st century BC.

Testament (Assumption?) of Moses, 1st century AD.

Testament of Abraham, 1st to 2nd century AD.

To this list (for a fuller examination of their contents see pp. 37–59) we may add, as has already been suggested, material found among the Dead Sea Scrolls.

(c) Methodology

Alongside the prolific output of scholarly works on the Old Testament pseudepigrapha in general and the Jewish apocalypses in particular, have gone new methods of analysis which have brought new light to bear on the apocalyptic texts themselves and also on the milieu from which they originally came. Of particular importance from the point of view of methodology has been the application of literary and sociological analysis. New insights have been gained as a result into the meaning of apocalyptic and into the influences that gave it birth. Most scholars, however, would recognize the provisional nature of their findings, not least in terms of the historical origins of the several writings and their place within the culture of the days in which they were written.

Scholarly investigation has over recent years addressed itself to a number of identifiable problems in this connection. One of these relates to the actual origins of apocalyptic: when did it first appear and under what circumstances and among what people did it emerge? What was its relation to the Old Testament prophetic and wisdom traditions? And is its use of mythology to be understood primarily in terms of predominantly Israelite culture or by reference to foreign influence? Such questions will be asked and answers sought in the next chapter. At this point we address ourselves to a second question – the definition of such terms as 'apocalypse', 'apocalyptic', 'apocalypticism' and 'apocalyptic eschatology' and the use of literary analysis as a tool with which to identify what is termed 'apocalyptic literature'.

3. A QUESTION OF DEFINITION

(a) A confusing situation

Throughout this book the expression 'apocalyptic' is used not only as an adjective but also as a collective noun, in common with traditional usage, to signify both the 'apocalyptic literature' as generally understood and that complex of ideas which produced it. This is done in full awareness of the fact that such usage has been given as one of the reasons for the confusion that has entered into the apocalyptic debate in the course of the years. Thus, J. J. Collins gives three reasons of which this is the first: the use of 'apocalyptic' as a noun to signify an amalgam of literary, social and phenomenological elements; the fact that the genre 'apocalypse' was not clearly recognized or identified as such in antiquity; and the fact that the apocalypses themselves often include various distinct literary forms such as visions, prayers, testaments, legends and so forth.[10]

The confusion to which reference is made is all too evident and has led to serious attempts to define such terms as 'apocalyptic', 'apocalypticism', 'apocalypse' and 'apocalyptic eschatology' – a task which, as the attempts have shown, is not at all an easy one. It may be true that, in some circumstances, 'to define' is 'to confine' and so to limit rather than to increase understanding. Nevertheless, the need to define such terminology, or at least to try and set out its parameters, has been deemed altogether necessary. Whether such attempts have in fact been successful is perhaps still open to question.

(b) The listing method

One approach to the problem which has met with severe criticism – and rightly so – is the so-called 'listing method' which seeks to define apocalyptic in terms of its marks or characteristics. Thus J. Lindblom suggested the following formal marks of apocalyptic literature as: 'transcendentalism, mythology, cosmological survey, pessimistic historical surveys, dualism, division of time into periods, teaching of the Two Ages, numerology, pseudo-ecstasy, artificial claims to inspiration, pseudonymity and esotericism'.[11] In one of my earlier books,[12] I added to this list a number of 'incidental' characteristics and suggested that four other more substantial marks might be identified: the apocalyptic literature is esoteric in character, literary in form, symbolic in language and pseudonymous in authorship. The difficulty of this approach is that such characteristics appear also in books that are not generally regarded as apocalyptic, and not all such characteristics appear in books that are so regarded!

(c) A literary phenomenon

Klaus Koch[13] brought a measure of clarity to this rather confused situation by distinguishing between 'apocalypse', to be defined in terms of literary type or genre, and 'apocalyptic', to be understood as 'an intellectual movement'. He took as his standard of measurement those apocalyptic writings composed in Hebrew and Aramaic, or else clearly expressing such influence, which he identified as Daniel, I Enoch, II Baruch, IV Ezra, the Apocalypse of Abraham and the Book of Revelation. These writings, when subjected to tests of a form-critical kind, conveyed the impression that 'there really was something like an apocalyptic type of writing around the turn of the era, i.e. the apocalypse was a recognizable literary type, albeit complex in character, absorbing into itself other component genres'. 'Apocalyptic' on the other hand is to be understood as a collective term indicating a historical 'movement of mind', the motifs of which can be identified, though not as easily as the form-critical marks of the apocalypse, as a literary type. These motifs he describes in terms of the impending overthrow of all earthly conditions in a great cosmic catastrophe as the climax of the predetermined course of history in which the 'angels of the nations' play an important part; beyond this catastrophe awaits a paradisal salvation for the righteous which issues from the throne of God and becomes visible as 'the Kingdom of God' on earth or as 'the age to come' over against 'the present age'. This final redemption is often associated with 'a mediator with royal functions' and is described as one of 'glory' in which the resurrected dead will share and which will characterize the age-to-be in heaven itself.[14]

(d) A three-fold division

P.D. Hanson[15] questions this analysis and proposes instead a three-fold division: apocalypse, apocalyptic eschatology and apocalypticism. The *apocalypse* is a literary genre to be found alongside other genres such as the testament, the salvation-judgment oracle and the parable used by apocalyptic writers. *Apocalyptic eschatology* (closely associated with prophetic eschatology) is described as 'a religious perspective', i.e. it is 'a way of viewing divine plans in relation to mundane realities'. It is not the exclusive property of a single religious or political party or group, but can be adopted by different groups or individuals at different times and in varying degrees. *Apocalypticism* is defined as 'a religio-social movement' which adopts the perspective of apocalyptic eschatology; but since such a 'movement' expresses itself in different ways as a result of changing historical conditions, it is not possible to give 'one formal cognitive definition of apocalypticism'. It is not as much concerned with 'systematic consistency' as it is with 'the demands of the immediate crisis'. Its net, as it were, sweeps up different themes, traditions and genres so that 'the result is often a collection of concepts and motifs which is highly eclectic in nature and characterized by the esoteric, the bizarre and the arcane'.[16]

This three-fold division is criticized in turn by M. A. Knibb[17] who expresses doubt that a clear distinction can be made between 'apocalyptic eschatology' and 'apocalypticism'. Even if such a distinction is made apocalypticism is not separable from the apocalypses themselves but must be approached through them. It seems to him best to work with a simple two-fold distinction, that between the apocalypses and apocalyptic eschatology. This same conclusion was put forward a few years earlier by Michael Stone[18] who suggested the abandonment of the terms 'apocalyptic' and 'apocalypticism' and the retention of the expression 'apocalyptic eschatology' alongside that of 'apocalypses'.

(e) A theological concept

Christopher Rowland takes the debate a stage further by urging that the essential character of apocalyptic is to be found, not in its literary form and not in any distinctive subject-matter such as that of eschatology, but rather in the disclosure of divine secrets through revelation:

> We ought not to think of apocalyptic as being primarily a matter of either a particular literary type or distinctive subject-matter, though common literary elements and ideas may be ascertained. Rather the common factor is the belief that God's will can be discerned by means of a mode of revelation which unfolds directly the hidden things of God.[19]

But, almost inevitably, this approch has also met with criticism. In claiming 'divine disclosure' rather than 'eschatology' as central to apocalyptic, it is argued, Rowland cuts out a number of books generally recognized as apocalyptic such as the War Scroll from Qumran. The questions remain: How is apocalyptic related to eschatology? And, is revelation-as-vision the 'essence' of apocalyptic?[20]

(f) Apocalypse: an attempted definition

Much work has been done on the apocalyptic literature by a group of American scholars in the SBL Genres Project.[21] There Collins examines the features of those writings usually regarded as apocalypses and on this basis offers the following comprehensive definition of the genre:

> 'Apocalypse' is a genre of revelatory literature with a narrative framework, in which a revelation is mediated by an otherworldly being to a human recipient, disclosing a transcendent reality which is both temporal, insofar as it envisages eschatological salvation, and spatial insofar as it involves another, supernatural world.[22]

Subtypes, he suggests, are detectable within this genre. Most significant is the distinction between, on the one hand, those which survey history leading up to an eschatological crisis but without reference to an otherworldly journey, and on the other hand those which describe otherworldly journeys and which may refer to historical review or cosmic phenomena or the fate of the individual after death.

This line of approach, then, claims that the *apocalypse* is an identifiable genre which nevertheless shares some of its important characteristics and motifs with other related literary genres represented, for example, in the pseudepigrapha, the Qumran Scrolls and the New Testament which can also legitimately be designated 'apocalyptic literature'. On such an understanding, 'apocalyptic literature' does not have a common literary form 'since apocalyptic utilizes all the old traditional genres, transforming them into new, and often hybrid forms'.[23] *Apocalyptic eschatology* is the predominant theme of the apocalypses and is to be distinguished from prophetic eschatology by its emphasis on the consummation of history rather than the course of history as the locus of 'the last things'.

(g) Conclusion

These, then, are some among many attempts that have been made in recent years to sort out an obvious confusion that has crept into scholarly debate. It cannot be said that complete clarity has been achieved or that a secure basis has been laid for future investigation. Doubt remains not only about the use of the word 'apocalyptic' itself, but also about the recognition of the apocalypse as an identifiable literary genre and the acceptance of eschatology as its central theme, a theme it shares with other genres besides. Further work needs to be done, not least in an examination of apocalyptic as a theological concept and in a more thorough exegesis of the texts themselves. No doubt the researches and the debate will continue.

At the risk of making confusion worse confounded, let me try to sum up my own tentative understanding of the situation:

By *apocalypse* I mean (following the definition given by J.J. Collins) a literary genre which, though covering a wide range of topics, has a particular interest in details of the heavenly world, the course (if not the content) of Jewish history and the destiny of the world and individuals within it, and claims that this has been given as a direct revelation from God by means of dream or vision or by the agency of angels.

By *apocalyptic* I understand a certain religious perspective or complex of ideas exemplified by the apocalypse and related literature, a perspective that is wider than that of eschatology but is characterized by a peculiar preoccupation with 'the last things' and the coming judgment, and wider too than those books designated 'apocalypses', being recognizable also in writings of a related kind.

By *apocalyptic eschatology* I mean that expression of belief about 'the last things' to be found in those writings that reflect the apocalyptic perspective. Prophetic eschatology and apocalyptic eschatology are related to each other in terms of origin, but are to be distinguished from each other in at least two respects: whereas the former perceives salvation in communal terms of the nation or the righteous remnant within the nation, the latter perceives it also in terms of the individual; and whereas the former is focussed on the earthly scene and the restoration of Israel, the latter is focussed on a transcendent world involving an afterlife of bliss and coming judgment.

II

Apocalyptic: Its Birth and Growth

I. APOCALYPTIC AND ITS HISTORICAL BACKGROUND

(a) 'Tracts for the times'

The apocalyptic books of the so-called intertestamental period can truly be described as 'tracts for the times' in the sense that they constitute a record of the years c.250 BC to c.AD 100, not in terms of historical event only, but in terms too of the response of faith which the nation of Israel was called upon to make when faced with crisis and tyranny of many kinds. They cannot be properly understood apart from the religious, political and economic circumstances of the times, nor can the times themselves be understood apart from these books whose hopes and fears echo and re-echo the faith of God's people. They reveal the inner side of that conflict which continued almost unceasingly throughout these three whole centuries. The apocalyptic literature is essentially a literature of people who saw no hope for their nation simply in terms of politics or on the plain of history. The battle they were fighting was on a spiritual level, against 'spiritual powers of wickedness in high places'. And so they were compelled to look beyond history to the dramatic and miraculous intervention of God who would set to rights the injustices done to his people. The expression of such a belief is often fanciful and exaggerated, to our way of thinking; but book after book throbs with the passionate conviction that all that God had promised would surely come to pass. Apocalyptic is often described as a literature of despair; but with equal appropriateness it could be described as a literature of hope: God would

14

vindicate his people once and for all and bring to its consummation his purpose and his plan for all the ages.

(b) Hellenistic culture and Jewish hope

There was, as we shall see, a long period of gestation prior to the birth of such apocalyptic writings as I Enoch (in part) and the Book of Daniel, probably in the third and second centuries BC. It is still a matter of debate whether certain earlier canonical writings should be designated 'apocalyptic' (see pp. 19f. below) or whether they should be regarded as 'embryonic', not yet fully developed. What is clear is that the 'intertestamental' years, and the century or so that preceded, were marked by the remarkable growth of that hellenistic culture so dear to the heart of Alexander the Great (336–323 BC) and his successors, and that Jewish apocalyptic is, to a marked degree, a protest against many of the values which that culture represented.

Alexander set himself the task of bringing into one the civilizations of East and West on the basis of that Greek culture which he himself had inherited and of which he was the avowed champion. In his triumphant march eastwards towards India, national, political and cultural barriers were thrown down so that people of quite different backgrounds were made to feel that they belonged together within 'the inhabited world' (*oikumene*). He set himself to teach Greeks and Asiatics, for example, to accept each other as partners in a common culture by establishing Greek cities and colonies all over his great Empire. The rapid spread of *koine* (or 'common') Greek facilitated this process of hellenization. All told, it was an age marked not only by cultural but also by religious syncretism which caused great anxiety among some at least of the Jewish community.

Beneath the surface of this syncretistic Hellenism the old Eastern religions of Babylonia and Persia continued to exercise a powerful influence. This is not surprising, for when Alexander took over the Persian Empire (which itself had taken over the Babylonian Empire) and pressed on towards India, the breach he made in the barrier separating East and West made possible an intermingling of cultures which was to have a profound effect on the life and religion of the Jewish people throughout the Dispersion which embraced all but Jerusalem itself.

Under Alexander's immediate successors, the Ptolemies and the Seleucids, a policy of toleration was for the most part pursued, allowing Judaism and Hellenism to co-exist. Far from being encouraged by such an attitude, however, many Jews who were jealous to maintain the tradition of their fathers saw in the exposure of their religion and culture to Hellenism a major threat to their very existence. Their sense of apprehension was deepened still further by the fact that the promises made by God through his servants the prophets had not materialized. The Golden Age to which they had pointed with such assurance was slow in coming, and now these prophetic voices had long since fallen silent and prophecy itself was deemed to be dead.

It was a time of great soul-searching. The promises of God through his prophets and the promises of Hellenism through its culture were diametrically opposed – or so it seemed to many devout Jews. A choice had to be made: there were some who opted for the fashionable culture with its promise of a new day of enlightenment and freedom, but there were others who were utterly convinced that the promises of God made of old would indeed be fulfilled and his Kingdom would come. What is more, they would be fulfilled, not in the far distant future, but in the immediate present. The quite obvious contradiction between such a hope and the events of history, not to mention the actual happenings of life around them, put such men under severe pressure. They could find no solution to the problem, save one – God himself would intervene in judgment and establish his messianic rule once and for all, a Kingdom in which his enemies would be destroyed and Israel would receive the dominion and the power for ever.

This was the conviction and the message of the apocalyptic writers. The voice of prophecy might well have fallen silent, but they believed that they themselves were inspired by God to interpret the prophets' message to their own generation and so, in a sense, were in their true line of succession. With confidence they asserted that the Day foretold by the prophets was indeed upon them and that today marked the *kairos*, the decisive and appointed hour. This assertion was confirmed, not just by pointing to divine acts of deliverance within history, but by disclosing divine revelations affirming such deliverance beyond history.

Alexander had a plan to unify all humankind in one 'inhabited world'; but God, they believed, had an even greater plan, to unify all human history and indeed the whole cosmos in a unity which would find expression and fulfilment in the coming of his Kingdom when the people of God would at last enter into their promised inheritance. In the expression of such a hope, earth and heaven merge, as it were, into one, the immanent and the transcendent coalesce, the future promise becomes the present reality. In the words of André Lacocque,

> the very *raison d'être* of apocalyptic is the conviction that God has a plan to unify human history, a plan that needs to be discovered, for it constitutes the secret of the universe. In this fashion history is both polarized by a final and historical coming, and suspended in the eternity of divine knowledge and wisdom. That is why the kingdom of God transcends history, but is inserted into history in the reign of the saints (Daniel 7).[1]

(c) Antiochus IV and the Book of Daniel

Matters came to a head in the time of the Seleucid ruler Antiochus Epiphanes IV (175–163 BC) when the apocalyptic Book of Daniel was born. Fearful of the break-up of his kingdom, he instigated a vigorous policy of hellenization in an attempt to weld it more securely together. Socially and culturally the Jews must have been seriously affected. Some influences were quite insidious; others were quite open, as in the games held in the gymnasiums and amphitheatres where the participants were expected to share in the sacrifices offered to heathen gods.

When in due course Antiochus brought undue pressure to bear on the appointment of a High Priest of his own choosing, fighting broke out in the city. The king resented this challenge to his authority and determined to teach the Jews a lesson. He desecrated the Temple and plundered its treasures, and in 167 BC issued a decree forbidding the people to live any longer acording to their ancestral laws. The distinctive marks of the Jewish faith were proscribed on penalty of death and, to crown this infamy, an altar to the Olympian Zeus was set up on top of the altar in the Temple and swine's flesh offered on it (II Macc. 6.2; Dan. 11.31, 12.11).

It must have seemed to many that the experience of the Exile in the sixth century BC was taking place all over again in the second century. But, as then so now, there was hope of deliverance. As then so now 'the arm of the Lord' would be revealed (cf. Isa. 53.1). God would deliver his people and establish his Kingdom. In such circumstances it was altogether fitting that such a message of hope should be conveyed in the story of a wise and righteous man, Daniel, who, in the days immediately following the Exile, was himself given such re-assurance by divine revelation – the Kingdom would be given to 'the people of the saints of the Most High' (Dan. 7.18).

(d) Hasmoneans and Romans

The story of the Maccabean Revolt and the rededication of the Temple in 164 BC is a familiar one. The Hellenizers seemed to have been thwarted. But in truth we see in the successors of the Maccabees, the Hasmonean House, the corroding influence of secularization and hellenization. And when, in course of time and with the help of the Romans, the power passed into the hands of Herod (37–4 BC) and his sons, the policy of hellenization went on at an even greater pace. The rise of the Zealot party exemplified the burning hatred felt by many Jews for Herod and his family and also for the Roman procurators (AD 6–66) who in due course governed the land. To them and to many others the struggle was a holy war which reached its terrible climax in the so-called Jewish War of AD 66–70 when Jerusalem was destroyed and the Jewish state ceased to exist.

Throughout this whole period the Jewish nation passed from one crisis to another and earlier expectation of the coming Kingdom remained unfulfilled. The apocalyptists' hope, however, was not dashed, only deferred. And so book after book appeared, defying the tyranny of rulers and the pressures of a society that would deny the faith of their fathers and make a mockery of the coming Kingdom. These apocalyptic writings were indeed 'tracts for the times', both a protest and an affirmation that evil would in the end be destroyed and good prevail.

The fall of Jerusalem in AD 70 marked a crisis much greater than any that had gone before since the days of the Exile itself. This is reflected in such books as IV Ezra and II Baruch whose authors, in what has been described as a theophany, grapple with the tragedy that had befallen Jerusalem and its people and try to find an explanation for it. The two writers follow different paths, but their responses are essentially the same in the end – there is no solution to be found in this present world order, but only in a future order when proper retribution will be made and justice done.

The apocalyptic writings, then, reflect the times in which they were written and contribute their own understanding of these times in a cry of despair which is also an assertion of hope that 'God in heaven will establish a kingdom which will never be destroyed, nor will it ever pass to another people; it will shatter all these kingdoms and make an end of them, while it will itself endure for ever' (Dan. 2.44 REB; cf. Rev. 11.15).

2. THE ROOTS OF APOCALYPTIC

(a) Apocalyptic and prophecy

It has been argued by many scholars that the primary influence on Jewish apocalyptic was that of Old Testament prophecy. I myself have described it as the 'taproot' from which apocalyptic drew its nourishment, enabling it to come to full-flower around the beginning of the second century BC.[2] It has come increasingly to be recognized, however, that the actual origins of apocalyptic go much further back than the second century BC and that prophetic eschatology was a most creative factor in the process of development.

This is clearly expressed by P.D. Hanson[3] who affirms that 'apocalyptic is the mode assumed by prophetic eschatology once it has been transferred to a new and radically altered setting in the post-exilic community'.[4] Otto Plöger, who shares this same judgment[5] traces the origins of apocalyptic to the prophetic eschatological hopes of the fifth century BC and through such writings as Isaiah 24–27, Zechariah 12–14 and Joel 3–4 to its full flowering in Daniel in the second century BC. Hanson likewise looks to the late prophecy of Israel – from the sixth century BC onwards – for evidence of the transformation of prophetic eschatology into apocalyptic. Thus he can describe Deutero-Isaiah as 'proto-apocalyptic', Isaiah 24–27, 34–35, 60–62 and Zechariah 9–10 as 'early apocalyptic' (late sixth century), Zechariah 12–13 as 'middle apocalyptic' (first half of the fifth century), and the framework of Trito-Isaiah and Zechariah 11 as full-grown apocalyptic

(475–425 BC). In setting out this line of progression from prophecy to apocalyptic he calls as witness not only the eschatological content of these prophecies, but also the several genres of literature which they represent. Both Plöger and Hanson, then, root apocalyptic firmly in prophetic eschatology and push back its origins to a time much earlier than the second century BC to which these origins have been traditionally ascribed.

An interesting contribution to this debate has been made by R.E. Clements[6] who, together with a number of other scholars, recognizes that 'a substantial layer of apocalyptic elaboration and re-working of earlier prophecy' is to be found embedded in the pre-exilic prophetic books such as those of Isaiah, Ezekiel and the Twelve Prophets. He illustrates this by reference to the occurrence of the phrase 'a full end is decreed', to be found in Isaiah 10.23 and Isaiah 28.22 which, he argues, are late editorial comments, markedly apocalyptic in character, and again in Daniel 9.27. On the basis of these passages he asserts that the apocalypses arose out of a re-working of earlier prophecy, re-applied and re-issued. These prophecies were believed to contain knowledge concerning the mysteries of future judgment for Israel and the nations, and essentially took the shape of an apocalyptic-type eschatology. Such a development points to the literary character of apocalyptic which took shape when it was placed in the hands of the scribes. This agrees with the judgment of Lars Hartmann who describes apocalyptic simply as 'prophecy among the scribes'.

(b) Apocalyptic and wisdom

But the view that apocalyptic derives ultimately from prophecy (however different and distinctive it may have become in its subsequent development) has been seriously challenged, not least by G. von Rad[7] who claimed that pride of place must be given to 'wisdom' as the soil from which apocalyptic grew, albeit with help from certain foreign sources. He pointed to the fact that in the apocalyptic books from the second century BC onwards very few, if any, prophets are named as the putative authors or heroes, whereas men like Daniel, Enoch and Ezra are counted among 'the wise'. Moreover, such books are concerned not just with history but also with nature and with the cosmos – the changing seasons, the movements of the heavenly bodies, geographical and meteorological interests, etc. – matters which are a concern of wisdom. When they do relate to history, their contention that it is predetermined by God in prescribed divisions of time leading up to the end and the introduction of a transcendent world order, is altogether different from that of the prophets who regarded the plain of history itself as the arena in which God made himself known in his saving acts. This concept of predeterminism is not characteristic of prophecy, and the interpretation of history in terms of dreams and visions, so common in the apocalyptic writings, is a function of 'the wise man'. From such arguments as these he concluded that the matrix from which apocalyptic came could not be that of the prophetic tradition but rather that of wisdom itself.

This conclusion, however, has not been found altogether convincing by many scholars for a number of reasons.[8] One is that the subject of eschatology, which is so prominent in the apocalyptic writings and also in the prophets, is, in the wisdom tradition, conspicuous by its absence. A second is that there is really nothing in the wisdom literature which corresponds to that determinism set forth so clearly in apocalyptic; it is true that there is a considerable difference in this regard between apocalyptic and prophecy also, but there is a recognizable relationship between them in, say, Deutero-Isaiah with its references to Yahweh's overruling purpose in history and his fore-knowledge of events. Besides this, there are many other close similarities between apocalyptic and prophecy, and it is surely significant that the apocalyptists themselves recognize the interpretation of the prophetic writings to be a key function of their calling.

(c) Apocalyptic and scribalism

But even though it may be argued that the primary influence on the emergence of apocalyptic was that of prophecy rather than that of wisdom, this does not mean that apocalyptic is to be identified with prophecy or indeed to be divorced from wisdom. It seems clear that, although apocalyptic may well owe its origins to prophecy, in the course of its development it came to be deeply influenced by other factors besides, among them the widespread Babylonian scribalism of the hellenistic period which was encyclopaedic in its interests[9] and that mantic or divinatory expression of wisdom which showed such great interest in dreams and visions.[10] Within this scribalism much speculation was in evidence concerning the ordering of creation, the 'sciences' of astronomy, astrology, cosmology and cosmogony, the movements of the heavenly bodies and the secrets of creation contained in heavenly tablets. The scribes themselves were men of learning and experience who set great store by study and travel and an understanding of ancient lore. They set themselves to update and re-interpret earlier oracles and omens by techniques of interpretation which find close parallel in Jewish apocalyptic. J.Z. Smith concludes, from a study of scribalism in Egypt and elsewhere during the hellenistic period, that 'apocalypticism is a learned rather than a popular religious phenomenon. It is widely distributed throughout the Mediterranean world and is best understood as part of the inner history of the tradition within which it occurs rather than as a syncretism with foreign (most usually held to be Iranian) influences'.[11]

In this connection it has been customary to draw a fairly sharp contrast between Greek and Hebrew modes of thought. The consensus of scholarly opinion now is that, though there are indeed important differences between them in, say, the area of eschatology, there is nevertheless much more common ground than has sometimes been acknowledged. The indications are that Jewish apocalyptic was influenced by hellenistic/oriental thought during the intertestamental period, but this is not to say that it can be regarded as in any substantial way a foreign implantation in Hebrew soil.

In this description of the development of apocalyptic in Judaism two metaphors have been used. One has been from gardening: the seeds were sown at an early date, but it was not until the third or second century BC that the 'full flower' appeared. The other has been from biology: the period of gestation was long, the embryo was recognizable for what it was, and in due course the child was born! Some have called it 'the child of prophecy'. Others have been less sure. P.D. Hanson, for example, identifies its mother as prophecy, but has hesitations about the identity of its father! R.P. Carroll suggests that 'perhaps he should seek the father among the wisdom circles of ancient Israel'.[12] Hanson indeed himself suggests that wisdom may have been wedded to apocalyptic eschatology in the third and second centuries BC; but (changing the metaphor) he sees in

Daniel, for example, 'one station along a continuum reaching from pre-exilic prophecy to full-grown apocalyptic, very much at home on Jewish soil and manifesting foreign borrowing only as peripheral embellishments'.[13] Whatever the parentage of apocalyptic may be, Hanson has gone far towards demonstrating not only that its chief source is to be found in prophetic eschatology but also that the apocalyptic 'perspective' may be traced back to the sixth or fifth centuries BC. The apocalyptic literature which emerged in the third or second century BC onwards may claim to stand in the same lineage, but it is a complex creature owing much to its parentage, but owing something too to the environment and culture within which it was reared.

(d) Apocalyptic and the priesthood

Before looking more closely at that environment and culture in which apocalyptic may have been conceived and within which it developed to its full expression in the third or second century BC, there is one other matter that deserves comment: the relationship between apocalyptic and the priestly tradition.

At first sight any such connection might seem quite tenuous, given for example the priests' disinterest in the question of eschatology and the antagonism which for so long scholarly opinion believed to exist between the prophet and the priest in Old Testament times. This latter assumption is now no longer to be given credence, particularly where the post-exilic period is concerned.

On the contrary there are quite positive signs throughout the apocalyptic writings that indicate the influence of the priestly tradition behind apocalyptic in general and a number of the apocalyptic books in particular. One of the most obvious indications of this is to be found in the Qumran community which was a priestly body both in origin and in practice, and yet was essentially apocalyptic in its religious expression.

Interest in matters of a priestly or cultic kind is well illustrated also in a number of other apocalyptic works. This is to be seen, for example, in such a book as that of Daniel which lays emphasis on the importance of dietary laws (cf. 1.8ff.), and also of the centrality of the Temple and its sacrificial system (cf. 8.11, 14; 9.27). In this connection we may observe the important place given to the Book of Daniel within the life of the Qumran community. Other apocalyptic or related-apocalyptic books convey the same impression. Most obvious among these is the Book of Jubilees whose author, there is reason to believe, was himself a priest. (We observe that Levi is exalted above Judah, chs 31–32, and the secret tradition to be passed on is placed in the hands of Levi's descendants, cf. 45.16.)[14] So too with the Testament of Levi which clearly reflects priestly concern, and II Enoch which, in its concluding section (chs 68–73), traces the priestly line of succession from Methuselah to Melchizedek, outlining in legendary form the origin and development of the priesthood as a holy institution.

Another factor pointing in the same direction is the place given in the apocalyptic writings to the importance of astrology and numerology and the part these play in calendrical calculations so crucial for the fixing of the various religious festivals.

Besides all this, there is the likely influence on apocalyptic of mantic wisdom which, as we have observed, is closely associated with the priestly office and which 'specializes' in the interpretation of dreams and visions (a feature of apocalyptic). Indeed, there are a few instances in the apocalyptic writings where priestly divination is referred to favourably as is the practice of the sacred lot (cf. Jub. 8.11) and in the reading of 'the signs' in the severed pieces of a sacrificial beast (cf. Apoc. of Abr. 15.9ff; II Bar. 4.4).

(e) Apocalyptic and culture
It will have become clear that the influences bearing upon the growth of apocalyptic and the emergence of the apocalypses themselves must have been many and varied. In the earlier books such as I Enoch and Daniel Babylonian and Persian influences are no doubt to be detected alongside biblical traditions which in turn reflect Canaanite traditions. At a later time, as illustrated by the Testament of Abraham, Greek influence is more noticeable. The hellenistic age with its admixture of traditions and beliefs representing both east and west provide the matrix from which in due course emerged a literature which was at one and the same time distinctive, reflecting the Jewish religion and culture, and yet in many ways a product of the heterogeneous population of the Mesopotamian world. Peter R. Ackroyd sums up

the situation in these words: 'External influence may make itself felt, but internal developments are also of very great importance. In the event, there is likely to be a subtle inter-relationship between the two'.[15]

Of significance in this regard is the part played by mythology in the Jewish apocalyptic books which, though it may appear to the modern mind at times quite bizarre and fantastic, represented in ancient civilizations the 'acceptable' language and thought-form of religion. It speaks graphically of a cosmic realm over against the 'real' world of historical event which is celebrated and whose traditions are re-enacted in the cult. It has been argued by an increasing number of scholars that the mythical traditions celebrated in the Jerusalem Temple, and which find illustration in the Book of Psalms, for example, were in a revived and revised form influential in the thinking of late Hebrew prophecy and thereafter found vivid expression in Jewish apocalyptic. On this ground, it is claimed, there is no need to look to, say, a Persian source to explain the origins of such mythological expression: there is no need indeed to look beyond Israel's own history and tradition and the old Canaanite myths which lie behind them.[16] Of particular interest is the fairly frequent reference in these writings to themes from the ancient royal cult and the myth of a warrior God. This had been regarded with grave suspicion by the pre-exilic prophets, but in post-exilic times, with the demise of earthly kingship in Israel, the notion of divine kingship gained in favour, as illustrated in its use by Deutero-Isaiah (cf. 42.10–16, etc.). The theme is taken up by the apocalyptists and becomes a prominent feature in their writings as in the Book of Daniel. There the whole of history is presented in terms of a conflict between God and those who would lay claim to his royal throne. The fact of God's kingship is emphasized as is the enthronement of his agent, the 'son of man', surrounded by a royal retinue of holy angels (cf. Dan. 7). So too with the First Book of Enoch where the 'throne-visions' show God seated on his kingly throne, again surrounded by his angel hosts (I En. 14; cf. also Test. of Levi 5; II En. 20–21; Apoc. of Abr. 18). The myth-image shows variations, reflecting no doubt something of the culture of the day, but its origins can no doubt be traced back to such passages as the story in I Kings 22 and the visions contained in Isaiah 6 and Ezekiel 1. It reappears fairly frequently in

Christian apocalypses, as in Revelation 4, and later on plays a significant part in the so-called *Merkabah* (throne-chariot) mysticism.

3. THE BIRTH AND GROWTH OF APOCALYPTIC

The origins of Jewish apocalyptic are wrapped in mystery. Help, however, has been provided over the years, by the application of methods of analysis adopted by sociology and social anthropology which attempt to answer the question: What is the socio-historical context out of which the apocalyptic 'perspective' may have grown? Scholarly attempts to answer this question have proceeded along a number of lines, a few of which may be considered here.

(a) Conventicles in Israel

Otto Plöger,[17] for example, looks to the post-exilic community established under the influence of Ezra and Nehemiah for an answer. This was a theocratic community which recognized in the restored Temple and in its liturgy the only *eschaton* that really mattered. Within such a community and in face of such fulfilment, there was no room for the national eschatological hopes expressed by the prophets.

This assumption, however, was challenged by certain groups or 'conventicles' within the nation who were still convinced of the relevance and validity of the prophetic word. They were vitally interested in the ancient prophetic writings and more especially the eschatological utterances they contained which depicted a glorious future for the people of God. Their hopes for the future which became more and more focussed on divine intervention at the *eschaton* were different from those of the popular national eschatology which saw deliverance in terms of military force. In some such way, says Plöger, prophetic eschatology developed into apocalyptic eschatology.

He sees this trend emerging in the fifth century BC and continuing right down to the second century BC, being influenced in the process by foreign religious ideas, with matters coming to a head in the troubled time of Antiochus Epiphanes. At that time the eschatologically-orientated group was represented by men called by the name Hasidim or Pious Ones (to whom reference is made in I Maccabees 2 and elsewhere, see pp. 30ff below) whose convictions, he claims, are expressed in the Book of Daniel. At the beginning, these Hasidim sided with the Maccabees in their military struggle against Antiochus; but soon they withdrew their support and looked, not to armed struggle for their salvation, but to the direct intervention of God and his promised Kingdom. In some such way the eschatological hopes of the ancient prophets developed into the dualistic-eschatological hopes of the apocalyptists.

Plöger's attempted explanation has not been found altogether satisfactory by many scholars, if only because the second of his two groups is too vague and he is unable to identify who its members were within Jewish society.

(b) Two rival factions

P.D. Hanson's approach differs from that of Plöger in a number of respects, but the basis of his argument is essentially the same.[18] He too traces back the origins of apocalyptic well before the rise of Daniel to the prophets of the exilic and post-exilic periods.

He points out[19] that, although the pre-exilic prophets lived in 'a mythopoeic religious environment' in which the divine activity was recognized as occurring on a cosmic plain, they themselves interpreted this activity in terms of and within the context of the movements and events of history, i.e. (to use modern jargon) they 'historicized' it or 'contextualized' it. They spoke of standing in God's 'heavenly council' to hear his word, but that word was directed to the hard facts of life as they knew them. Thus, in the pre-exilic prophets, cosmos and history, vision and reality, were held together in tension.

This tension was subsequently maintained by Ezekiel who was able to integrate his strange and sometimes bizarre visions of the cosmic Yahweh into the events of current history. But even here there are evident signs that a change is taking place which finds expression in Deutero-Isaiah and, even more markedly, in Trito-Isaiah. Deutero-Isaiah, under pressure from the soul-destroying experience of the exile, makes use of the old conflict myth, so common it would appear in the days of the monarchy, to express his belief in God the Creator and Redeemer of the universe. The tension between the cosmic vision and the realities of this world is still maintained, but there are indications that prophecy, as previously understood and practised, is about to undergo a radical change.

That change is clearly marked in Trito-Isaiah where, according to Hanson, apocalyptic was born. 'Prophetic eschatology', he concludes, 'is transformed into apocalyptic at the point where the task of translating the cosmic vision into the categories of mundane reality is abdicated.'[20] The visionary-followers of Deutero-Isaiah, becoming increasingly pessimistic about the state of the world in which they lived, thought of their coming salvation less and less in terms of historical reality and more and more in terms of that timeless, cosmic plain which offered escape from this present age into a new creation in which the cosmos would return to its primaeval state. Such a development took a decisive step in the direction of a dualistic view of the world and a belief in great world-epochs – two prominent features of apocalyptic. In this way, says Hanson, apocalyptic eschatology was born. Its origins are to be traced back to prophetic eschatology whose language and imagery is to be seen as a 're-mythologizing' of a 'long-since demythologized religion'.[21] It is not dependent on 'outside' influences such as that of Persian thought, but can be explained adequately in terms of native Israelite tradition.

Hanson finds the socio-historical setting for such a development in two parties which, he reckons, began to emerge between the years 538 and 500 and which came to form rival factions: a Zadokite-led group whose hopes were based on the programme set out in Ezekiel 40–48, and a mixed group comprised of followers of Deutero-Isaiah and dissident Levites. The former group, under Persian patronage, sought to re-establish the Temple cult and so to restore the land as the dwelling-place of Yahweh; the latter (minority) group maintained the visionary hopes expressed by the prophet of the exile and longed for Yahweh's intervention to bring about the defeat of their enemies. He sums up the situation neatly by claiming that 'if apocalyptic was conceived in Ezekiel, manifested its first contractions in the destruction of the temple, and was carried to full term in exile by Deutero-Isaiah, it was born shortly after the *gola* in Third Isaiah'.[22] Third Isaiah reflects a situation 'so pessimistic that the mundane order assumed a guise unsuitable for their restoration hopes'.[23] The temptation of the minority group was to look away from the mundane sphere to the cosmic realm for evidence of salvation – from historical reality to mythical vision. Thus the delicate balance maintained by Deutero-Isaiah was upset, and less attempt was made to interpret their visions of Yahweh's plans in terms of historical realities. This process, as we have seen, is traced in a 'continuum' from Third Isaiah through the 'Isaiah apocalypse' in Isaiah 24–27 and Zechariah 9–14 right down to the Book of Daniel. Such continuity, however, is not to be seen in terms of a continuous visionary *party*, but rather in terms of a visionary *perspective* finding expression in different groups in post-exilic times.

Hanson's analysis, however, has met with criticism from a number of scholars. Thus R.P. Carroll[24] complains that his definitions of prophetic and apocalyptic eschatologies are unclear and controversial; the motif of the divine council as a central factor in all the prophets is also far from clear as is his 'attempt to translate the decisions of the divine council into historical, political and human terms'.[25] He questions also Hanson's 'excessive use of polarization' which leads to false antitheses, such as that between myth and history, and to an over-simplified presentation of material that is much more complex than Hanson allows. He questions too his treatment of myth itself and the manner of its presentation which implies that prophecy is to be seen in relation to history, and the cult is to be seen in relation to myth, whereas both prophecy and cult exist in history and operate with mythical concepts and motifs. André Lacocque takes this criticism a bit further by saying that Hanson's asserted 'opposition between a royal and priestly theology on the one hand and a prophetic theology on the other is too radical' and gives it as his judgment that 'in the time of the apocalyptists, as in the pre-exilic and exilic periods, eschatology sprang from the cult'.[26]

M.A. Knibb,[27] in his criticism, concedes that there is 'a considerable element of truth' in what Hanson says, but asserts that there is a great deal of uncertainty not only about the dating but also about the sequence of the several prophetic oracles to which he refers, and at the same time he questions the contextual-typological method which he adopts. He recognizes that the Jewish apocalypses may well represent a continuation of Old Testament prophecy just as apocalyptic eschatology may well represent a continuation of prophetic eschatology, but asserts that there are other influences besides the prophetic which contribute to their emergence, and that in particular the apocalypses are to be recognized as 'learned compositions standing within a learned tradition'.[28]

(c) Groups and parties: 'the wise' and the Hasidim

Attempts have been made to identify the several apocalyptic writers with specific parties that emerged in Israel early on in the intertesta-mental period. Thus, the Essenes have been seen as the source of hopes and expectations expressed in a number of these books as in the Scrolls from Qumran. In the case of others, links have been found with the Pharisees, and in other cases with the Zealots. But the probability is that they are not to be traced back to any given party at all but, at different stages, have emerged from quite diverse groups, known and unknown, and from men who owed no allegiance to any party at all.

There were, as we shall see, certain strongly marked traditions such as that associated with the name of Enoch where we can detect a common theological outlook. But different theological outlooks are expressed in other apocalypses such as in IV Ezra and II Baruch which reflect a different setting and different circumstances and address themselves to different problems. But whilst it is true that the apocalypses represent no single identifiable movement or community within Judaism, they nevertheless share a common conviction (that they are recipients of an important and inspired revelation), a common purpose (to assure and encourage their people when faced with whatever crisis might confront them) and a common hope (the imminent coming and triumph of God's Kingdom over evil of every kind). They might differ considerably in terms of social and religious groupings, but the very names by which they were known was an indication of their common task: they were the Elect, the Righteous, the Saints, the Poor and the Wise.

This last designation is a particularly interesting one. In the Book of Daniel, for example, reference is made to the *maskilim*, 'those who are wise' (11.33, 35; 12.3, 10), whose responsibility it is to instruct the *rabbim*, 'the many', so that they in turn may become wise. It would be wrong, at this stage in its historical development, to see in the word any reference to a specific group or party, although in course of time it came to signify a particular class of learned men as at Qumran, for example, where the word *maskil*, 'wise one', is used as the title of an official.

'The wise', then, were in all probability a rather small elite, a spiritual aristocracy as it were, who believed they had been given special insight into the hidden mysteries of God and his universe. They were apparently a learned group of men who laid great store by tradition and Torah, who had searching and inquisitive minds and who, in course of time, came to engage in much speculation, particularly of an esoteric kind. It is difficult to identify them much more precisely from the information we have. But we may have just a hint in a description of the ideal scribe given by Ben Sira (himself a scribe) in chapter 39.1ff. of his book. The scribe, he says, is 'the wise man' who studies in the school of wisdom to uncover her secrets for those who would seek her illumination. These are his words:

> He will seek out the wisdom of the ancients
> and will be occupied with prophecies;
> he will preserve the discourse of notable men
> and penetrate the subtleties of parables;
> he will seek out the hidden meanings of parables,
> and be at home with the obscurities of parables.

E.W. Heaton indicates that it would be wrong to urge an identity of outlook between Ben Sira and, say, the writer of Daniel – they were men of different temperaments, living in very different times, even though only a few years apart. But what is astonishing, he says, is 'not the difference between the two works, but the fact that their common tradition was strong enough to make them comparable . . . Ben Sira and the author (of Daniel) stand for two different emphases among the scribes . . . Fundamentally they are brother doctors of the same divinity'.[29] It may well be that the author of Daniel who, like the hero of his book, was numbered among 'the wise', came from the scribal circle and that others of the apocalyptic writers belonged to the same ilk.

But is it possible to identify these 'scribes' somewhat more clearly? A number of scholars have seen the author of Daniel as belonging to that group of men called Hasideans (in Greek) or Hasidim (in Hebrew) who are reckoned to be forerunners of the Pharisees and the Essenes, two parties within Judaism that emerged at a later date. Our knowledge of the Hasidim is extremely limited, being confined to three references in I Maccabees 2.42; 7.12–13 and II Maccabees 14.6 and possibly also Jubilees 23.16 and I Enoch 90.9–11. In I Maccabees 7.12 they are named alongside 'the scribes', with whom they are probably to be identified, and include in their number members of the priestly class. Such association with scribes and priests would seem to strengthen the claim that the author of Daniel, with his emphasis on wisdom and priestly ritual, may have belonged to their number. One objection to this assumption has been the image of the quietist *maskilim* in Daniel which clashes with that of the Hasidim presented elsewhere as 'mighty warriors of Israel' (cf. I Macc. 2.42; 7.13; II Macc. 14.6–7; Pss. Sol. 16). This, however, is not an insuperable difficulty if, as is thought, they began as quietists (cf. I Macc. 2.29–37) but were forced to change their stance and join the rebellion against Antiochus as a result of his dire persecution.

They were pious men, as the very name implies, dedicated to the defence of the Law, who later withdrew their support from the Hasmoneans once religious liberty had been achieved. Even if it be conceded that the author of Daniel may have belonged to the ranks of the Hasidim, it has to be said that relatively few of the apocalyptic books, such as the Apocalypse of Weeks and the Animal Apocalypse in I Enoch together with the Book of Jubilees, are compatible with the little we know about this body of 'pious men'. The fact remains that the bulk of the apocalypses have no one specific source but represent a fairly wide spectrum of social grouping within Israel at that time.

4. ITS 'POPULARITY'

We have seen reason to believe, then, that the apocalypses were the work of learned men who were counted among 'the wise' and were familiar not only with the Law and the tradition of the fathers but also with the 'wisdom' of the age in which they lived, with its ancient traditions and secret lore.

Apocalyptic was not a 'popular' literature in the sense that it was written for the masses. The actual circulation of the books would be very limited, but it is safe to say that the ideas contained in them must have been much more widespread than the literature that contained them. We have to remember, too, that behind the books lay a long and varied tradition or rather, long and varied traditions, some of which we shall consider presently. Much of that tradition would be, and would continue to be, oral and would readily become part of the popular deposit of pious religious belief. Restricted, then, though the actual books may have been, their influence would make itself felt from an early date on the life of the Jewish people as a whole. The books themselves would find eager acceptance, particularly in times of tribulation or crisis, causing new ones to be written and old ones to be revamped.

Many were written in Palestine either in Hebrew, the tongue of the learned of that day, or in the vernacular Aramaic. Others were written in Greek in the Dispersion. In course of time the Palestinian apocalypses found their way into the Dispersion also where they were translated into Greek and won popularity among the Jews there. In Alexandria particularly they would receive acclaim and come to have a much wider public than they ever had in Palestine itself.

One sign of their subsequent popularity is to be found in the great number of languages into which they were in due course to be translated – Latin, Syriac, Arabic, Ethiopic, Coptic, Slavonic, Georgian and so forth. This wide range of translations no doubt reflects the degree of popularity they came to have among the Christians, but may reflect also the place they held at an earlier date within Judaism itself.

In course of time the apocalyptic books fell out of favour with the Jews. No doubt it was felt that some features highlighted by them were inimical to the accepted practice of Judaism in the post AD 70 era, and the rather 'revolutionary' teaching of some may have been regarded as too dangerous in the changed circumstances of the nation. But the chief factor would no doubt be the adoption and adaptation by the Christian church of many Jewish apocalyptic writings whose messianic and eschatological teachings were eminently suitable for the purpose of Christian propaganda. Whatever the reasons may have been, the fact is that the apocalyptic books have survived for the most part, not in the original Hebrew or Aramaic, but in Greek or in the many other languages to which reference has been made and that, apart from the Book of Daniel which was early enough and popular enough to gain recognition as sacred scripture, the tradition of apocalyptic is in fact Christian and not Jewish. Some of the books were taken over just as they were. Others were made more suitable for their purpose by Christian editors who interpolated new material expressing specifically Christian allusions. More than that, they began to produce apocalyptic writings of their own which, together with those of Jewish origin, continued to exercise a considerable influence. By far the most significant of all the Christian apocalypses is the canonical Book of Revelation which draws freely on Jewish tradition and in which some Christian scholars have found a Jewish nucleus in Christian guise. Like the earlier Jewish apocalypses, a number of these books are known to us only by name or in fragmentary allusions. In due course, like their Jewish precursors but for different reasons, they too fell out of favour and, with few exceptions, disappeared as valid writings of the Christian church.

III

Apocalyptic Groups and Apocalyptic Books

1. APOCALYPTIC GROUPS

We have already observed that, during the intertestamental period, there were many splinter groups within Judaism throughout Judaea and beyond and that the composition of apocalyptic literature was not confined to any one of these. One such distinct group was that at Qumran which not only valued apocalyptic writings from outside its own immediate circle, but also wrote apocalyptic-style books themselves. The indications are that there were other groups besides, much less easy to identify, who also expressed their hopes and fears in the form of books of an apocalyptic kind. Three such groups, it has been suggested, may be indicated in the books we know as I Enoch, Daniel and Jubilees.

These three had much in common with the Qumran community as evidenced by the numerous portions and fragments of these works found in the remains of the library there and by the fact that, in the case of I Enoch and Jubilees, they shared the same sectarian calendar which was followed zealously at Qumran. They had much in common too with one another by the very fact that they shared the apocalyptic-approach. And yet the differences between them are such as to suggest that these three writings may well have been the product of three distinct groups within Judaism.

The evidence of I Enoch points to the existence of one such group within which the book, in its several parts, was both produced and preserved. In 93.10, for example, reference is made to 'the chosen

35

righteous from the eternal plant of righteousness' where a 'righteous group' within the 'righteous nation' is indicated. This same designation, 'the righteous', is used elsewhere in the book, as in the Similitudes, with the same connotation – a recognizable group eager to perpetuate the tradition associated with their forefather Enoch, a tradition which was to continue and to find expression in later books like II Enoch and III Enoch. This impression of a distinct group behind I Enoch finds support in the fact that, as in the Book of the Heavenly Luminaries, emphasis is laid on the acceptance of a solar calendar. We shall see presently that, in its origins, this 'Enoch tradition' is in all probability of pre-Maccabean vintage and goes back to a much earlier date than had been previously thought.

It is less certain that any such distinct group lay behind the Book of Daniel whose style and approach suggest that it is from a quite different apocalyptic 'stable' from that of I Enoch. In its origins however, as we have seen, it has a close affinity with the *maskilim*, 'the wise', in the time of the Maccabees whose wisdom found expression in the court-tales of Daniel 1–6. Its particular brand of apocalyptic expectation is different from that of I Enoch as indeed it is also from that of Jubilees, pointing to a different origin and background.

The Book of Jubilees shares much of the traditional thinking of both I Enoch and Daniel, but once again there are distinct differences, indicating different origins. These differences are particularly marked by its pronounced *halakhic* emphasis in its application of the Mosaic law and by its developed dualism in which demonic agencies feature prominently. On both these counts, as in its emphasis on the solar calendar already referred to, it has much in common with the community at Qumran, although there is no hint of the existence of an organized community such as theirs.

In this chapter we shall examine these three apocalyptic books emanating, as it would seem, from three quite different backgrounds, if not groupings, and thereafter look, more briefly, at some of the other apocalyptic writings.

2. I ENOCH (ETHIOPIC BOOK OF ENOCH)

(a) A popular book

Apart from a few references to his lineage, all that we know of Enoch from the Old Testament is that he 'walked with God, and he was not, for God took him' (Gen. 5.24).[1]

It is not at all surprising, however, that, in course of time, this mysterious figure with his miraculous entry into heaven should become the focus of all kinds of speculative and legendary material concerning the spiritual world where God lives together with his holy angels. There is ample evidence to show that in the post-Old Testament period such Enoch material not only grew but also became extremely popular within Judaism and, even more so, within Christianity.

The immense interest within early Judaism in the 'Enoch tradition' (as also in the accounts of that other antediluvian, Noah) is most evident in I and II Enoch, the Book of Jubilees and the Genesis Apocryphon from Qumran. These reveal what might be described as 'a secret tradition' associated with the name of Enoch which is both composite in character and highly complex. There he is presented as a wise man to whom the angels make known the secrets of the heavens and the natural order; he is a recognized authority in the science of astronomy and in the skilled work of calendrical calculations so important for priestly ritual; he is a priest who intercedes on behalf of fallen angels; he is a heavenly scribe, responsible for the divine records on the Day of Judgment, and he is called by the name 'son of man'. In course of time the tradition fell out of favour with the Jews, chiefly perhaps because Enoch had come to be held in such high regard by the Christian church. In Jewish mediaeval writings, however, he regained his popularity and was given what almost amounted to messianic honours.

Early Christian tradition also knew Enoch as an important figure and I Enoch as an important book. This is borne out by the testimony of Jude vv. 14 and 15 where he is described as a prophet who, 'in the seventh generation after Adam prophesied, saying, "Behold the Lord came with his holy myriads (of angels) to execute judgment on all, and to convict all the ungodly of all their deeds of ungodliness"'. This is a direct reference to I Enoch which was obviously regarded as a sacred writing of some authority. The writings of the Church Fathers, moreover, show that he was a popular figure throughout the Christian world in the second century. Beyond that date his significance decreased and he fell out of favour in the Church of the Western world. In Eastern Christendom, however, he continued to occupy a high place of honour. In a fourth century Coptic work, for example, the Apocalypse of Paul, it is Enoch who welcomes Paul into heaven (cf. II Cor. 12.2–4). And it is Enoch and Elijah, who are identified with the two witnesses referred to in Rev. 11.3–12, who resist the Antichrist and who are killed but raised to life again.

For quite a long time I Enoch was known (apart from brief allusions and quotations in other literature) only in an Ethiopic translation, having been discovered in Ethiopia in 1769. Hence the name often given to it – the Ethiopic Enoch. Since then a number of Greek manuscripts have also come to light. Then in the 1940s came the discovery of the Dead Sea Scrolls at Qumran among which were a whole mass of Aramaic fragments representing every section of the book except one, the so-called Similitudes or Parables of Enoch (chapters 37–71). It would seem likely that the original Aramaic document was translated into Greek which was in turn translated into the language of ancient Ethiopia. Thus I Enoch came to be preserved in the tradition of the Eastern Church and is held in high regard in that church today. It was not until 1912 that it became readily available in English through a translation by R.H. Charles.

(b) A composite work

I Enoch is a composite book in five parts, ranging in date probably from the third century BC to the first century AD.[2] In its final form it is artificially arranged in these five parts, perhaps on the analogy of the five books of the Pentateuch or the five books of the Psalms. These are generally identified as the Book of Watchers (1–36), the Book of Parables or Similitudes (37–71), the Book of Heavenly Luminaries (72–82), the Book of Dream Visions (83–90) and the Book of Admonitions (91–105), followed by a conclusion in chapters 106–108. We shall look briefly at each of these in turn and try to get a taste of the sometimes exotic fare set before us.

The Book of Watchers (1–36) is one of the earliest sections (together with the Book of the Heavenly Luminaries contained in chapters 72–82). It is usually dated near the beginning of the second century BC but, as we shall see presently, may date from the previous century. The writer presents himself as God's spokesman, claiming a divine revelation made known through a vision in which he foresees the judgment of the wicked and the justification of the righteous (1–5). There then follows a composite story which tells how 200 angels called 'Watchers' 'lusted after the beautiful daughters of men'. The children who resulted from their co-habitation grew up as giants whose spirits corrupted the earth. Enoch pronounces judgment on the fallen angels who will have no peace until the Final Judgment (12–16). He then visits their place of punishment and sees in Sheol the several compartments prepared for the wicked and the righteous corresponding to the degree of punishment or reward the dead will receive (17–36).

The Parables of Enoch (37–71) were probably at one time an independent book. There has been much debate about the date and provenance of these chapters and there is no small disagreement still among scholars. It is generally recognized, however, to be a Jewish work and is possibly to be dated around the middle of the first century AD and so prior to the fall of Jerusalem. It relates three Parables, each in the form of a vision in which Enoch is translated to heaven where he is introduced to revelations concealed from the eyes of mortal men. The first concerns the coming judgment of the wicked and discloses 'all the secrets of heaven'. The second introduces a figure called 'the Chosen One' who stands before 'the Head of Days' seated on 'his throne of glory'; he is referred to as a 'son of man' (46.4ff.), and in a passage reminiscent of the Suffering Servant in Deutero-Isaiah is seen as 'the light to the nations'; in the end he will be enthroned and, together with the righteous ('the chosen ones'), will inherit the earth. In the third Parable this 'Chosen One' is again placed on the throne of glory and is seen as judge of men and angels. (For consideration of the term 'son of man' see chapter 7.)

The Book of Heavenly Luminaries (72–82) is an astronomical treatise dealing with the measurement of time based on the movement of the sun, the reliability of the solar year of 364 days and an account of cosmic upheaval revealing the time of the end. The form it takes is that of a guided tour by the archangel Uriel through the heavens in which the order and the governance of the world are displayed. Blessings are recounted for those who know the right reckoning of the years and their intercalary days measured by the movement of the stars.

The Book of Dream Visions (83–90) is probably to be dated in the late 160s BC in the Maccabean period and consist of two visions about the future of the world. The first foretells its destruction by flood. The second outlines the history of the world from Adam to the Maccabees and declares the coming of the Messianic Kingdom. The description is given in symbolic language in which, for example, the fallen angels are depicted as falling stars and holy angels as men. Seventy angels, or 'shepherds' as they are called, set as guardian angels over the nations, exceed their authority and are duly punished. At last the new Jerusalem comes and with it God's Messiah.

The Book of Admonitions (91–105) may reflect the situation in the late Hasmonean period. Enoch's children are admonished to follow righteousness and their resurrection is predicted with the judgment of the wicked. Within this Book is the so-called *Apocalypse of Weeks* (93.1–10; 91.11–17), in which history is divided into ten unequal parts, seven of which are already passed and three of which are still to come. These remaining three will see the triumph of the righteous, the banishment of evil and the creation of an age that will have no end.

(c) A lost tradition

It has long been thought that I Enoch, in its earlier parts, might be older than the Book of Daniel, to be dated in the third rather than the second century BC. This contention has found support in the discovery at Qumran of many Aramaic fragments which, on palaeographic and other grounds, can be dated in that earlier period. These fragments, moreover, represent a larger text than that of the Ethiopic Enoch, suggesting that what we now possess may well be only part of a much larger and older Enoch literature.

It will have become clear from even a cursory examination of the book that I Enoch is very different in its expression from, say, the Book of Daniel with its emphasis on eschatology and 'the end of the age'. Here in I Enoch the approach is of a much more speculative kind, showing a deep interest in such matters as cosmology, astrology, astronomy, calendrical calculations and so forth.

Enoch himself is introduced variously as a wise man, a scribe and a priest. It is hardly likely that such identifications and elaborations could have grown simply out of the vivid imaginations of the apocalyptic writers meditating on Genesis 5.24. There are in fact certain clear indications pointing to a speculative tradition within Judaism going back to a time well before the intertestamental period, a tradition which was influenced in no small measure by Mesopotamian lore with its interest in astronomical, geographical and mythological concerns. In particular it may have drawn on that widespread mantic or oracular wisdom associated with Babylon which shows a tradition of learning on the part of a particular class of wise men whose chief concern was the interpretation of dreams and omens. This in turn is related to priestly concerns which involved the sacred calendar and the notion of the heavenly Temple, a notion to which reference is made in Exodus and in II Chronicles.

There are several other significant 'signposts' pointing to the early influence of Babylonian lore and legend on the growth of this speculative element within Judaism, detectable in the Enoch tradition. The 'scientific theories', for example, expressed in the Book of the Heavenly Luminaries (chs 72–82) reflect Mesopotamian ideas rather than the more advanced Greek science of the later hellenistic period. Besides this, the heavenly journeys made by Enoch in the Book of the Watchers reflect what Michael E. Stone calls 'a particular mythological map of the world . . . closely related to Mesopotamian geographic conceptions'.[3] These factors point to a learned tradition nurtured in certain Jewish circles in the third century BC if not before, reflecting Mesopotamian religion and culture.

Another pointer in the same direction is to be found in the figure of Enoch himself who may well have been patterned on certain Mesopotamian wisdom figures. Of particular interest is the early Babylonian tradition which refers to ten 'kings' who reigned before the time of the Flood, semi-divine beings who had come down from heaven. The seventh in line was Edoranchus who is no doubt to be identified with Enmeduranki, king of Sippar, the city of the sun-god Shamash. Shamash introduced Enmeduranki to the secrets of heaven and earth and taught him the art of divination. In course of time he became the founder of a guild of priestly diviners and passed on his secret knowledge to his descendants. There can be little doubt that the figure of Enoch came to be modelled on that of Enmeduranki. Thus, Enoch is seventh in line from Adam just as Enmeduranki is seventh in line from the first 'king' after creation. Enoch's life-span, moreover, is given as 365 years, corresponding to the number of days in the solar year and has a particular relevance to Enmeduranki who worshipped the sun-god Shamash. Besides this, Enoch's heavenly journeys and subsequent revelations of divine mysteries may also reflect Enmeduranki's introduction to the heavenly secrets, and his identification with a heavenly being in I Enoch 71.1 (a 'son of man', see pp. 125f.) may have some connection with the semi-divine character of the 'kings'. The Babylonian belief that the men who lived before the Flood were men of profound wisdom finds a clear echo, then, in the Jewish tradition concerning Enoch as also his great-grandson Noah.[4]

This Enoch tradition obviously differs from our received Old Testament in a number of significant respects. For example, it has no place for the elaborate sacrificial cult of the Temple and offers no great role to be played by the Law of Moses. Rather, it lays great stress on the Day of Judgment and the part played in this by the mediation of Enoch and the revelation vouchsafed to him. And now to these we can add those speculative interests of which there is ample evidence in I Enoch. We note that such matters as these have little or no mention in the traditions recorded in the Old Testament, not even in the Wisdom literature where we might have expected them to appear. In other words, no tradition, or group can be identified in the biblical sources which fostered this type of speculative wisdom.[5]

It is 'a lost tradition' for which there is no obvious evidence left in the text of the Old Testament. It has often been argued that Jewish apocalyptic was influenced directly to a quite considerable degree by foreign sources such as that of Persia and Zoroastrianism. Such a judgment has now to be considerably modified. It has become clearer that speculative elements like those to which reference has been made, deriving originally from Mesopotamia and elsewhere, may have become part and parcel of Israelite life and culture from an early date and may have been a feature of Israelite life even as far back as the time of the First Temple.[6]

We seem to have, then, in the Enoch tradition, as evidenced by I Enoch itself, the record of a very conservative Jewish group whose roots go well back before the Maccabean era and before the time of writing of the book itself in the third century BC, perhaps even to the days of the First Temple before the Babylonian exile. It represents a new style of apocalyptic writing in which the emphasis is laid, not so much on eschatology as on speculative and 'scientific' concerns. With the coming of the persecution under Antiochus and the troubles that followed, eschatology was to assume a more central role as evidenced by several books written around that time, chief of which was the Book of Daniel.

3. THE BOOK OF DANIEL

The Book of Daniel is fraught with many problems of a critical character which need not concern us here in any detail. We simply observe that it is in two parts (chapters 1–6 and 7–12), is written in two languages (Aramaic and Hebrew), reflects two backgrounds (the Dispersion and Palestine) and may have been composed by two (or more) authors.

(a) The name

The hero of the book, who is also its reputed author, is a man named Daniel from among the Jewish exiles in Babylon. The name appears several times in the Old Testament, but none of them has any direct reference to the Daniel of this book. Two such references, however, are of particular interest. One is Ezekiel 14.14, 20 where the name appears alongside Noah and Job, presumably as an antediluvian like them, and also in 28.3 where he is presented as a proverbially wise man. The other is Ezra 8.2 (together with Nehemiah 10.6) where 'Daniel' is given as the name of an otherwise unknown priest who, in the sixth century BC, returned from exile in Babylon. It would appear that the author(s) conveniently combined the figure of the legendary wise man of old with that of the unknown priest to serve the purpose he had in mind, namely to encourage the faithful in his own day (the second century BC) by means of prophecies purporting to come from an earlier day (sixth century BC) and to demonstrate by this means that the end of their troubles was at hand. His purpose would be doubly served in this way when we remember that the name 'Daniel' signifies 'God is the defender of my right' (cf. Gen. 30.6).

It is true that in Ezekiel the name is spelt 'Dan'el', but there can be little doubt that this is simply a different form of the same word. These three men – Noah, Daniel and Job – renowned for their righteousness and outstanding wisdom were not Israelite patriarchs, but rather holy men belonging to other nations, and the impression given is that they are here figures in a tradition or traditions wider than those of Israel itself.

This impression is strengthened by the occurrence of the name 'Dnil' (which may be vocalized as Dan'el or Daniel), borne by a king in the Ugaritic Tale of Aqhat discovered at Ras Shamra in northern Syria and dating from the fourteenth century BC. There it is said of him:

He judges the cause of the widow,
He tries the case of the orphan.

That is, he is a wise ruler renowned for his righteous acts. Taken in conjunction with the Ezekiel references this would indicate that, from very early times, there was a Phoenician-Canaanite legend concerning an ancient hero whose reputation for righteousness and wisdom was such that he was designated a man of renown.

There are indications, moreover, which suggest that this old legend may well have survived in different forms in Jewish lore. For example, one development of it may conceivably be reflected in I Enoch 6.7 and 69.2 where 'Dan'el' or 'Daniel' is the name given to one of the fallen angels, the 'wisdom figure' of old having assumed angelic status and then subsequently having 'fallen from grace'. Another development, it has been argued, may have gone in quite another direction finding its locus in Babylon with its world-renowned reputation for wisdom and finding expression in a collection of stories concerning one whose wisdom confounded that of 'the wise'.

There is no proof that the hero of the Book of Daniel was associated with the ancient Daniel or that the Ezekiel references were used in the ways just suggested. But the suggestion is at least plausible. Another 'pointer' in this direction is the reference in Jubilees 4.20 which states that Enoch married Edni 'the daughter of Dan'el, his father's brother', i.e. Dan'el is the uncle and father-in-law of Enoch and the great-great-grandfather of Noah.

The cumulative evidence, then, would seem to indicate that during the intertestamental period the story of an ancient hero, Daniel, renowned for his wisdom, was known in Jewish circles.

(b) A Daniel tradition?

Such knowledge, however, was not confined to the writings just mentioned. Indeed, there would appear to have been at this time a cycle of tradition concerning Daniel which found expression not only in the biblical narratives but also in the 'additions' to Daniel now contained in the apocryphal or deutero-canonical books – Susanna, Bel and the Dragon, and the Song of the Three Young Men. These are contained in the Greek translation of the Old Testament, but there is good reason to believe that some of them at least were originally written in either Hebrew or Aramaic[7] and were not necessarily composed under the inspiration of the canonical book itself.

These in turn have been supplemented by two works from Qumran – the so-called Prayer of Nabonidus and a historico-eschatological fragment designated 'Pseudo-Daniel'[8] – and also by the so-called Lives of the Prophets dating from the first century AD. The first of these works from Qumran refers to Nabonidus, the last Babylonian king and bears a close resemblance to the account of Nebuchadnezzar's miraculous recovery from illness as recorded in Daniel 4. The evidence is limited, but the indications are that, if there was not an actual 'Daniel tradition' at this time emanating from a 'Daniel group' of learned men (see pp. 30ff.), the Book of Daniel was part (albeit an important part) of a wider literature relating to a man of that name.

(c) The book

One of the first things that strikes the reader of Daniel is that chapters 1–6 are very different in their format from chapters 7–12. The former consist of 'court tales' or 'martyr legends' about Daniel and his companions in Babylon and are told in the third person; the latter describe a series of visions together with their interpretations, told in the main in the first person. The former reflect life under the Babylonian and Persian kings in the sixth century BC when the persecution of the Jews was no real problem; the latter reflect a time of suffering and oppression compatible with life under Antiochus Epiphanes in the second century BC. Despite these differences, however, the two parts form a recognizable unity, with chapter 7 serving as a bridge between.

This difference of format is matched by a difference of language, although these two do not coincide. Hebrew is the language used in the introductory section, 1.1–2.4a, and in chapters 8–12. The rest of the book is in Aramaic. It has been suggested that the author(s), around the year 165 BC, wrote up in the vernacular Aramaic the popular tales told in chapters 2–6 which had been passed down from earlier days, probably in oral form, and concluded his account with chapter 7 which, we note, has a lot in common with chapter 2. Thereafter, as a kind of commentary on chapter 7, he would record his visions of 'the end' and the coming Kingdom, contained in chapters 8–12, in the sacred language of Hebrew, attributing these to the hero of the stories, thus indicating a common authorship. Finally he would write in Hebrew an introduction to the whole up to the point where it is reported that the Chaldeans spoke 'in Aramaic' (2.4).

The two parts of the book, moreover, differ not only in their format but also in their content, though once again there is a unity that encompasses story and vision in one so that, although the word 'apocalypse' may be said to apply strictly to the visions in chapters 7–12, it can quite properly be used of the whole.

The stories, with their God-given dreams, had lessons to impart that would bring much encouragement to faithful and waverers alike in the time of the tyrant Antiochus: the wisdom God gives is far superior to that of the heathen; those who keep the Law of God will in the end reap their just and rich reward; kingdoms may rise and kingdoms may fall, but the Kingdom of God will last for ever and fill the whole earth; God has known the course of history from its beginning and knows too its end which is coming soon; he will preserve and reward those who continue to put their trust in him.

The lessons of the visions, though more cryptic, were no less telling: the Kingdom of God will replace the four 'bestial' empires from the time of Nebuchadnezzar to that of Antiochus (ch.7); the 'little horn' on the head of a ram, representing that tyrant, will be broken and utterly destroyed (ch.8); Gabriel affirms that Israel's seventy years' captivity would last for seventy 'weeks of years' (ch.9); the predetermined course of history from Cyrus to Antiochus has all been foreseen by God (chs.10–11); the rewards and punishments associated with the Kingdom will match the certainty of its coming soon (ch.12). The reader's expectation is highlighted by the author's device of transferring to an honoured figure in the past his own understanding of historical events so that the author's own account of the past is seen as the man Daniel's forecast of the future.

Enoch and Daniel, then, have much in common as apocalyptic writings: both appear to have legendary connections and both came to formation in the late Persian or early hellenistic period. But there are significant differences, not least in the form their 'revelations' take, whether as heavenly-ascents or as dream-visions, and also in their contents, whether in cosmological concern or in eschatological expectation. Such differences will be the subject of a later chapter and will illustrate still further the varied and complex nature of Jewish apocalyptic.

4. THE BOOK OF JUBILEES

(a) Its nature and origin

The particular genre of literature indicated by Jubilees is difficult to determine. Basically, however, it is a narrative *midrash*, a kind of 'running commentary' on Genesis and part of Exodus which makes ample use of *halakhic* and *haggadic* material to expound the text, i.e. it is particularly concerned with biblical laws, rites and ceremonies and expresses this frequently in the form of story and legend. As such it can hardly claim to be an apocalypse *per se*; but its understanding of revelation, its adoption of pseudonymity and its world-view generally (not least as set out in ch.23) all indicate that it can rightly be counted among the 'apocalyptic literature' which is not confined to the apocalypse-form but encompasses many different genres.

The origin of Jubilees is bound up with its date of composition, a quest which is greatly helped by the discoveries at Qumran not only of many fragments of the book itself but also of other related books such as the Genesis Apocryphon which is in all probability dependent upon it. There are many indisputable similarities between Jubilees and the Qumran literature, not only in terms of theology but also in practical matters, not only in the adoption of a common calendar but also in actual literary dependence, indicating the prior existence of Jubilees. But there are many differences as well which support the view that Jubilees could not have been written at Qumran. Perhaps chief among these is that, whereas the Qumran community had severed its connection with 'the establishment' and its priesthood in Jerusalem and withdrawn to the wilderness of Judaea, the Book of Jubilees gives no hint of any such breach but on the contrary was fully supportive of the establishment, i.e. Jubilees was probably written before the breach between the Maccabees and the Essenes which, it is reckoned, took place during the reign of either Jonathan or Simon (160 BC–130 BC). VanderKam, after a careful analysis of the historical, literary and theological connections, comes to the conclusion that Jubilees is most likely to be dated between 161 BC and 140 BC.[9]

O.S. Wintermute agrees with this judgment and claims that all the evidence identifies the author of Jubilees 'as part of a zealous, conservative, pious segment of Judaism which was bound together by its own set of traditions, expectations and practices' and points out that such groups played a significant role in the struggles of the Maccabean age. The author of Jubilees, he concludes, probably belonged to the Hasidic branch of Judaism which represented the spiritual genealogy of both the Pharisees and the Essenes.[10] He agrees with F.M. Cross that 'the concrete contacts between the editions of Enoch, Jubilees and the Testaments of Levi and Naphtali found at Qumran on the one hand and the demonstrably sectarian works of Qumran on the other, are so systematic and detailed that we must place the composition of these works within a single line of tradition'.[11]

(b) Its teaching

Written in Hebrew, Jubilees has survived as a complete book only in Ethiopic. It is given this name because it divides world history into specific pre-determined periods of time measured by 'weeks of years' and 'jubilees', a jubilee being a period of seven weeks of years, i.e. forty-nine years. According to M. Testuz,[12] a period of forty-nine jubilees represents a complete era of world history, the conclusion of which coincides with the giving of the Law on Sinai which thus marked the beginning of a new era. As we shall see, the giving and keeping of the Law was, to the writer, a matter of primary importance.

The book takes the form of a revelation vouchsafed to Moses on Mount Sinai, recorded by 'the angel of the presence' (1.27ff.), in which 'the Lord revealed to (Moses) both what was in the beginning and what will occur (in the future), the account of the division of all the days of the Law and the testimony' (1.4). What we have in Jubilees then, it is claimed, is 'a second law' corresponding to 'the first law' of the Torah (cf. 6.22) which expounds and applies that first law and relates it to contemporary life. The book is not just a repetition of the Genesis account with some incidental embellishments thrown in for good measure; it is a commentary on how life ought to be lived in contemporary society in the light of the eternal Law of God as revealed in the history of God's dealings with the patriarchs of old. That is, the book has a profound theological and practical intent.

The author, it would seem, belonged to a priestly family and laid great store by the law as it related, for example, to rites and ceremonies and to times and seasons. Though revealed to Moses, it is of eternal validity. Thus the law of the Sabbath is 'a great sign' (2.17), having been 'kept in heaven before it was made known on earth' (2.30). Likewise the law relating to circumcision: the very angels in heaven had themselves been circumcised 'from the day of their creation' (15.27); it was 'an eternal ordinance ordained and written in the heavenly tablets' (15.25). So too with laws relating to purification, intermarriage, the offering of sacrifices and the rest, all of which were being challenged in the writer's day as was the evil of nudity required of young men competing in the Games. All breaches of such laws are here condemned, and their strict observance by both angels and patriarchs held up as an outstanding example.

And as with rites and ceremonies, so too with times and seasons. To the writer of Jubilees, particular days had a particular religious significance, and so it was of the utmost importance that a given festival, for example, should fall each year on the same day of the week. This would be possible only by the adoption of a solar calendar of 364 days made up of 12 months of 30 days each, with an intercalary day introduced every three months. The adoption of any official lunar calendar consisting of only 354 days would lead to complete confusion and a violation of festivals and holy days. His concern was not simply a question of correct chronology; it was a matter of vital theology. The religious festivals and holy days received from their fathers had a divine origin (32.21ff.), had been practised by the patriarchs of old (6.17f.; 32.4) and had been passed down by them through the ages in sacred books (45.16). Here, then, is a powerful plea to a people, many of whom were tempted to compromise their faith and practice as Jews, to return to the law of God and to obey his commands.

Apart from chapter 23 and the reference to 'what will occur (in the future)' in 1.4, the writer shows little or no interest in eschatology. He is not concerned about any Messiah, and the 'messianic kingdom' he has in mind is very different from the cataclysmic event to be found in some apocalyptic writings; it will come rather by gradual process in a renewed heaven and earth in which God's people will grow in spiritual awareness as they give themselves to a study of the Law of God. Little is said about the afterlife, except that the spirits of the righteous will have much joy (23.31), and judgment will be the lot of sinful men (4.24) and fallen angels (5.10).

A significant feature of the book is its teaching concerning angels and demons and its dualistic understanding of the spiritual forces of good and evil. Satan is introduced under the name of 'Mastema', the prince of evil spirits. The angels are divided into several categories, with different functions to perform. Some are set over the forces of nature; others are sent to teach men various skills, to inform them of God's will, to reveal to them heavenly secrets, to resist the forces of evil and to guard the nations of the earth. The source of evil is traced back to those angels called 'Watchers' who, in lust, entered into union with the daughters of men and were thereafter 'bound in the depths of the earth' (5.1ff.). From the bodies of the children of this illicit union – the giants – came forth evil demonic spirits who are the cause of disease and tragedy of every kind. It is they and not God who, under the leadership of Mastema, are responsible for evil in the world. Thus, it was Mastema and not God who tempted Abraham to kill Isaac (17.15–18.13) and encouraged the Egyptians to pursue Israel (48.12). He, together with the demons and fallen angels, will in the end be destroyed (10.18; 33.29).

The book is written with authority by one who represents, not a small sectarian group isolated from 'the house of Israel', but the priestly orthodoxy of his day. He recognizes the dangers facing Judaism from the encroaching hellenistic culture within which it is placed and, with good reason, warns against the temptations which it brings.

5. OTHER APOCALYPTIC BOOKS

We have seen, then, that in the older traditions represented by books like I Enoch and Jubilees the eschatological element is not at all prominent. This emphasis became more pronounced in the time of persecution under Antiochus and in the subsequent Maccabean struggle as illustrated by books like Daniel and the Testament of Moses. In the years leading up to the destruction of the Second Temple in AD 70, however, the old speculative emphasis reasserts itself so that we find a renewed interest in such matters as astronomy, astrology, heavenly journeys and zodiacal signs, particularly in those books written in the Dispersion. Yet another stage is reached in the years following AD 70 when we find, in the words of M.E. Stone, 'a final body of writings . . . (which) form a separate distinct group (such as II Esdras and II Baruch), distinguished by their preoccupation with the problem of theodicy, formulated in highly theological terms. Their central concern is to understand how God's justice evinces itself in the world, particularly in view of the destruction of Jerusalem and the Temple'.[13]

We shall examine these and other related matters in a later chapter, but in the meantime we shall glance at just a few of the remaining apocalyptic writings. The dates of a number of these are a continuing subject of debate as are their places of origin.

(a) The Testament of Moses

This book, like that of Jubilees, represents the outlook of Palestinian Judaism. There are serious differences among scholars concerning its date of writing, the two most favoured possibilities perhaps being the Maccabean period and the early years of the first century AD. It consists of a farewell address given by Moses to his successor Joshua in which he describes the events between the entry of the tribes into Palestine and the time of the end. Having spoken of the fall of Jerusalem, Moses goes on to prophesy the return from exile as a time of great apostasy (5.1–6; 7.1–9) and great suffering for God's people (6.3–9; 8.1–5) in which the reader readily recognizes the apostasy of the hellenizing priests of the Maccabean (or Hasmonean?) years and the suffering and torture inflicted on faithful Jews which finds illustration in the case of one Taxo and his seven sons who were willing to die rather than transgress the commandments of God (9.7). Such suffering precipitates the intervention of God and the coming of his Kingdom: 'His Kingdom will appear throughout his whole creation. Then the devil will have an end' (10.1). No earthly Kingdom is apparently envisaged; rather, Israel will be raised to 'the heaven of the stars' (10.9).

Unfortunately the extant manuscript is incomplete, breaking off in mid-sentence at 12.13. It has been suggested that this lost ending may have contained an account of Moses' death and bodily assumption to heaven, of which we learn elsewhere, and that the Testament might more accurately be called the Assumption of Moses to which reference is made in ancient sources. R.H. Charles has suggested that these two works may in fact have been combined. There is no way of proving or disproving this; but the matter is of peculiar interest because of the reference in Jude 9 to a dispute between Michael and Satan over the body of Moses, an account which may have come from the lost ending of the Testament or from the Assumption itself or perhaps simply from oral tradition.

(b) The Testament of Levi 2–5

The origin and composition of the Testaments of the XII Patriarchs, with its obvious Christian interpolations, present a difficult problem. The book as a whole builds on the account in Genesis 49 concerning Jacob blessing his children and on Moses' last words so as to give teaching on ethical and eschatological affairs. Of special importance in this latter connection is the Testament of Levi which, in its form and content, is closely related to the apocalypse genre. It is not too clear what the exact relationship is between the received text and the fragments of Levi-material found at Qumran.

The revelation of which the Testament speaks comes in the form of a dream-vision in which he is transported to the heavens where he is addressed by an angel: 'Then sleep fell upon me and I beheld a high mountain, and I was on it. And behold, the heavens were opened, and an angel of the Lord spoke to me' (2.5–6). There then follows a description of the several heavens through which Levi passes, with an explanation of their contents and functions. Originally, it would appear, three such heavens were envisaged (cf. II Cor. 12.2), but these were subsequently increased to seven, influenced no doubt by the Babylonian observation of the seven planets. Two of the seven heavens are perhaps of particular interest, involving as they do two concepts familiar to us from other apocalyptic writings: in the second heaven preparations are already being made for the Day of Judgment when vengeance will be taken on 'the spirit of error and of Beliar' (3.3), and in the seventh heaven Levi is confronted by the glorious throne of God (3.4).

The purpose of this heavenly journey is to confirm Levi in his God-given priesthood (5.2). He is to declare God's mysteries to men (2.10) which is his priestly prerogative. In this, as in other respects, the Testament of Levi has something in common with the Book of Jubilees.

(c) II Enoch (Slavonic Book of Enoch)

The patriarchal ascent through the seven heavens to the glorious throne of God is again the theme of II Enoch which, though it shares some of the ideas contained in I Enoch, does not necessarily belong to the same line of tradition. Once more the question of date is difficult;

it may belong to the first century AD and is available in a shorter and in a longer recension. It has a dual interest in cosmology and eschatology, these forming the content of a revelation made known to Enoch in the course of his heavenly journey.

In chapters 1–37 Enoch is taken up on the wings of angels to the first heaven with its 200 angels who govern the stars (4.1) and on to the seventh heaven where he beholds God on 'a supremely great throne' (22.2) and becomes himself 'like one of the glorious angels' (22.10). He records all these things in 366 books and takes this record back with him to earth for the encouragement of those who have survived the Flood.

In chapters 38–66 he returns to earth where he recounts what he has seen, including the fate of the wicked in hell and the peace of the righteous in Paradise. He exhorts his children to support the needy and so escape the judgment of God. Having addressed Methuselah and the elders of the people he is again taken by angels back into heaven.

In chapters 68–73 the people express the hope that a priest will be raised up in succession to Enoch. Methuselah, in a vision, sees himself crowned for this office, and the priestly line is then traced from him to Melchizedek. The latter's miraculous birth is then described and he is adorned in priestly garments. The book then ends with his departure to Paradise on Gabriel's wings.

The longer recension sees Enoch proceeding to an eighth and a ninth heaven which is the dwelling place of the twelve signs of the zodiac, and finally to the tenth heaven where he beholds 'the Lord's face, like iron made to glow in fire . . . ineffable, marvellous and very awful, and very, very terrible' (22.1).

(d) The Treatise of Shem

This small book is not an apocalypse, but it may be included here for reference as 'a related work',[14] dating perhaps from the closing years of the first century BC. It is noteworthy by reason of the fact that its twelve chapters follow the twelve signs of the zodiac and demonstrate how deeply astrology had penetrated into the thinking of Jews in Egypt during this period. Much is made of the influence of the heavenly bodies on natural phenomena and on human affairs. Thus, in 5.1 it is said: 'And if the year begins in Leo, there will be spring rains, then the soil will be deprived of the north winds.'

We are reminded of the part played by astrology and astronomy as a vehicle of revelation even in a community like that of Qumran which could produce a cryptic astrological document like the 'Midrash of the words of Moses'. The occurrence of such references illustrates a considerable imbalance in this connection within Judaism, this Treatise for example standing in marked contrast to, say, the Book of Jubilees with its strong anti-astrological stance (cf. 8.2ff.; 12.16ff.). But the author of the Treatise is himself ambivalent even within his own writing for, whilst taking his lead from the stars, he nevertheless asserts his faith in 'the living God' (8.2; 12.9).

(e) The Apocalypse of Abraham

This book is probably to be dated towards the end of the first century AD and, in its imagery, seems to draw on the tradition of I Enoch. Its theme is that of Israel's election and God's covenant with Abraham. Chapters 1–8 describe Abraham's opposition to idolatry; chapters 9–32 contain the apocalypse proper. In it God speaks to Abraham in a vision and thereafter he is taken up into heaven by the angel Yaoel, carried on the wings of a pigeon and a turtledove. There he is shown, among many 'great things', the dwelling-place of fiery angels (15.4ff.) and the chariot-throne of God (18.1ff.). From this lofty height Abraham sees the earth and its inhabitants and the coming judgment brought about by idolatry. The end of the present age, which is to last for twelve 'periods' (29.2), is close at hand. At its close will come the final judgment and the redemption of the righteous. The Gentiles will be afflicted by ten plagues; then God will send his 'chosen one' (31.1) who will gather together his scattered people, and the Temple with its sacrifices will be restored.

(f) The Testament of Abraham

This book survives in two recensions. It is a Jewish work with Christian interpolations and may date from the late first or early second century AD. In Recension A Abraham is presented as a good man who is nearing the end of his days. Michael is sent to bid him prepare for death, but Abraham is reluctant to give up his soul. He asks that he might first be allowed to see 'all the inhabited world' (9.6A) and this request is granted. He is lifted up 'on a chariot of cherubim' so that he 'soared over the entire inhabited world' (10.1A). So incensed is he by the sinfulness of mankind that he calls down fire from heaven. But God turns him aside from inflicting further punishment.

Abraham is then taken on a tour of heaven where, among other things, he sees the places of judgment. He is shown a broad way and a narrow way along which the souls of men must pass. They are tried by fire, by recorded evidence and by being weighed in the balance in three judgments – by Abel, by the tribes of Israel and by God himself (12.1–13.8A). Through intercessory prayer a soul whose good deeds and bad deeds are equally balanced is able to enter Paradise (14.1–8A). Abraham is thus encouraged to pray for the repentance of those he had previously condemned.

He then returns to earth to prepare his will and to make arrangements for his death. The fearsome angel Death appears in disguise to the reluctant Abraham who refuses to go with him. But by deception Death has his way and Abraham's soul is carried off to heaven by the angels and his body is buried at the Oak of Mamre (19.1–20.11A).

(g) The Apocalypse of Zephaniah

This apocalypse, whose date of origin is quite uncertain but which is generally reckoned to be the first century BC or the first century AD, has come down to us in greatly abbreviated form from three separate sources. It takes up the familiar refrain of a cosmic journey with an angel guide who reveals to the prophet, in his travels through the heavens, a series of seven self-contained episodes in which, *inter alia*, he sees the glories of heaven and the torments of hell. The writer describes various scenes relating to the heavenly Jerusalem and others relating to Hades. There he is confronted by 'the accuser' who holds a book containing a record of men's sins. The prophet intercedes for those who suffer torment and prevails over the accuser. Then, putting on 'an angelic garment' he joins the angelic ranks and unites with them in prayer. The book ends with four 'trumpet scenes' which, with trumpet blast, celebrate his triumph over the accuser, the opening of heaven, the interceding saints and the coming wrath of God. The theme of judgment is prominent throughout, the angels escorting the souls of the ungodly to Hades and eternal punishment.

(h) IV Ezra (II Esdras)

This Jewish apocalypse, to be dated around AD 100, is contained in chapters 3–14, chapters 1–2 and 15–16 being Christian interpolations. It takes the form of a theodicy in which the writer, in the name of the biblical scribe Ezra, seeks justification for God's dealings with his people in their suffering in exile following the capture of Jerusalem, and engages in speculation concerning the future Kingdom, the world to come and the future of men and nations.

It is in seven sections and takes the form of seven visions. In sections one (3.1–5.20) and two (5.21–6.34) the problem is posed: how is it that a righteous God can allow the suffering of his people, given the fact that they had an evil heart which prevented them from doing good? and what is the lot of those who depart from this life? The archangel Uriel assures him that this present age is fast drawing to a close and that a new age is about to appear. Section three (6.35–9.25) continues the same theme and goes on to refer to the final judgment, the appearance of the new Jerusalem and the coming of the Messiah who will rule for 400 years. Then comes the resurrection and the revealing of Gehenna and Paradise. In the fourth section (9.26–10.59) an attempt is made to answer Ezra's complaint: a mourning woman representing the devastated Zion is suddenly replaced by the new Jerusalem. In section five (11.1–12.39) a re-interpretation is given of the vision in Daniel 7 – the Roman empire is depicted under the symbolism of an eagle with twelve wings and three heads, and the coming of the Messiah is proclaimed under the figure of a lion who destroys that empire and delivers the righteous. In section six (13.1–58) eschatological interests predominate: the Messiah is depicted as a transcendent figure rising from the sea who destroys his enemies and delivers the righteous. The seventh section (14.1–48) is in the form of an epilogue affirming God's justice and describing the writing by Ezra of the 24 (canonical) books, which had been destroyed by fire at the fall of Jerusalem, and the seventy 'secret' (presumably 'apocalyptic') books. Ezra declares God to be justified and offers his praise.

The author, then, writes to offer encouragement to his people in their suffering following the destruction of Jerusalem which was believed to be the result of their sin. It was unfair to hold Israel responsible in this way, unable as they were to refrain from sin. The solution offered points to an eschatological hope: in the time to come the wicked will be punished, men and nations alike; the righteous will be rewarded and the evil heart removed from them by the mercy of God whose promises to Israel will at last be fulfilled.

(i) II Baruch (Syriac Apocalypse of Baruch)

This apocalypse, written around the year AD 100, in the name of Jeremiah's scribe Baruch, also relates the fall of Jerusalem in 587 BC at the hands of the Babylonians and reflects its fall once more in AD 70 at the hands of the Romans. Like IV Ezra it too is a theodicy, but unlike IV Ezra it is a very long and complex document. Whilst making use of the vision *motif*, it expresses itself also in a variety of other ways – in speeches, lamentations, warnings, dialogues, letters and so forth.

The basic problem addressed is introduced in the opening dialogue between Baruch and the Lord (1.2b–5.4) – the announcement of the pending destruction of Jerusalem. This raises the question of the fate of Israel and the justice of God in punishing his own people whilst letting their enemies go free. God assures Baruch that it is he and not the enemy who will overthrow Jerusalem, and in any case it will be only for a time: the world to come is for the righteous, and the real Jerusalem is in heaven (4.1–7). The destruction of Jerusalem will but hasten the coming of the future age. Baruch's questions and his demand for judgment on God's enemies occupy the rest of the book.

Twelve disasters will come upon the earth, but these will be followed by the coming of the Messiah, the resurrection of the dead and the final judgment (26.1–30.5). In a vision concerning a forest, a cedar, a vine and a fountain he learns of the destruction of the Roman empire: 'at the time of the dominion of the Messiah' the enemy will be uprooted (36.1–46.7). He is assured that everything is determined by God (47.1–48.50). Then, in response to Baruch's request, God shows him the nature of the resurrection body and the future of the righteous and the wicked after death (49.1–53.7).

Another vision follows showing a great cloud which pours out alternately dark water and clear water on the earth: by this means God makes plain to him the course of world history which will culminate in the coming of the Messiah and his Kingdom (53.1–74.4). Once again, as in IV Ezra, we see theodicy interpreted in terms of eschatology. The rest of the book contains admonitions to the Jews in the Dispersion to obey God's commandments and to trust in him (78.1–87.1).

IV

Revelation: Its Reception and Expression

1. INSPIRATION AND REVELATION

(a) Voice of prophecy dumb

The apocalyptists lived at a time when it was popularly believed that prophetic inspiration had ceased and the voice of prophecy was dumb. The writer of I Maccabees, for example, indicates that many years had passed by since a prophet was last seen in Israel (9.27) and expresses the hope that the day will speedily come when God will renew the gift of prophecy as a prelude to the coming of the Messianic Kingdom (4.46; 14.41). The Jewish historian Josephus confirms this belief in his day, indicating that the prophetic tradition that had begun with Moses had come to an end in the reign of Artaxerxes I in the fifth century BC. This, we note, coincided with the time of Ezra the scribe who, according to the biblical record, had brought back 'the Law Book' from Babylonia. The rabbinic sources are even more precise: the last of the prophets were Haggai and Zechariah, who had helped to build the Second Temple, and 'Malachi' who is regarded as their contemporary. With these prophets, then, and with Ezra the scribe (with whom 'Malachi' is sometimes identified) prophecy in Israel, it was believed, had come to an end.

(b) Revelation through Torah[1]

Reasons for the growth of such a belief are not too difficult to find. The hey-day of prophecy, it was thought, lay in the past, and ever since the return from exile it had been in rapid decline. There was no obvious correspondence, moreover, between the high hopes raised by prophecy and the events of their own day which, on the contrary, seemed to deny the erstwhile promises of a coming deliverance and the fulfilment of 'the messianic hope'. But more important still was the conviction, brought about by the canonization of the Pentateuch, 'the Five Books of Moses', that revelation found its embodiment and supreme expression in the written Torah made known to Moses on Sinai by divine inspiration and in due course renewed by Ezra the scribe. To many in Israel revelation was synonymous with Torah. Thus, Ben Sira likens it to Wisdom and refers to it as the supreme gift of God; the writer of the Book of Jubilees declares it to be perfect and eternal, and the writer of the Mishnah tractate *Pirke 'Aboth* affirms its basic role within God's vast universe: 'By three things is the world sustained: by the Law, by the (Temple)-service and by deeds of loving-kindness.' The Torah, then, contained everything that it had pleased God to make known of his mind and will. Torah and revelation were virtually one to which nothing could be added and from which nothing could be taken away.

But what about that oral law, that oral tradition, which had grown up alongside the written Law, with its multitude of new legal enactments interpreting and applying that Law to the life of the people? There could not be two *Toroth*, for revelation was one. The oral tradition, it came to be believed, carried with it the authority, not only of revered teachers, but also of a long line of tradition going right back to none other than Moses himself who was the source, not only of the written Torah, but also of the oral tradition itself. Together they formed a single revelation by means of which Israel could remain the covenant people of God.

(c) A new revelation: apocalyptic and Torah

The apocalyptists were every bit as devoted to the Torah as any other company of Jews at that time and to the revelation it expressed. This did not deny, however, that divine revelation could take complementary forms. They were in fact convinced that God had provided a new revelation for the days in which they were then living and that they themselves were the recipients and the agents of its disclosure. It was a 'dynamic' revelation that in no way ran contrary to the 'static' revelation of the written Torah. Both in fact came from the same source. They firmly believed that the revelation they recorded was by divine inspiration and was indeed a genuine revelation carrying with it divine authority.

In support of the validity of such 'dynamic' revelation the apocalyptists could make a strong appeal to the past – and they did! In ancient times, it was clearly reported in the Torah, God had made himself known in many different ways and to many different people – to patriarchs like Abraham, Isaac and Jacob, to great religious leaders like Samuel, Elijah and Moses, and to the prophets who, without a peradventure, declared 'Thus saith the Lord.' The apocalyptic tradition was like the oral tradition in that it too, could trace its ancestry to antiquity, to inspired men of old and indeed to Moses himself. But it was unlike that tradition in that it was not confined to the interpretation of pentateuchal laws nor need it seek to conform to any specific Mosaic formulation. It was 'new', moreover, in a sense that the oral tradition was not: not only did it come from the ancient past, it pointed forward also to the 'new age' that was soon to dawn.

An interesting commentary on this appeal to antiquity and the relation of the apocalyptic tradition to the Torah as divine revelation is given in the so-called 'Ezra legend', contained in IV Ezra 14 which apparently traces this tradition, like the oral tradition itself, back to Moses.

The chapter is in the form of a vision vouchsafed to Ezra the scribe who, like Moses of old, hears a voice speaking to him from 'out of a bush' (14.1). It tells him how God had led Moses to Mount Sinai where he revealed to him 'many wondrous things and showed him the secrets of the times and declared to him the end of the seasons', some of which he had to publish openly and others of which he had to keep secret (14.3–6). The meaning seems to be that God revealed to Moses at Sinai not only the Torah which was to be published, but a secret tradition also which was to be kept hidden – presumably the apocalyptic tradition with its account of great crises in world history and its indication of the coming end (14.10–12).

But according to Jewish tradition the record of this revelation – 'the things which have been and the things which will be' – had been destroyed by fire when Nebuchadnezzar captured Jerusalem in 587

BC (14.21). As a result of this, Ezra now offers to take Moses' place, as it were, and to write out 'everything that has happened in the world from the beginning' as well as 'the things that will be done' (14.21–22). To enable him in this task he asks for the inspiration of the Holy Spirit, and in answer to his prayer God gives him a cup 'full of something like water, but its colour was like fire' (14.39f.). He takes it and drinks, and thereupon his wisdom is increased, his memory sharpened and his mouth opened (14.40f.). Like Moses, he sets aside 40 days to receive and record what God will reveal to him. He dictates what he has heard to five scribes who record the revelation in 94 books (14.44). At the end of that time God again speaks: 'Make public the 24 books that you wrote first, and let the worthy and the unworthy read them, but keep the 70 that were written last, in order to give them to the wise among your people. For in them is the spring of understanding, the fountain of wisdom and the river of knowledge' (14.45ff.). The 24 books that are to be published openly are obviously those of canonical scripture, and the 70 that are to be kept secret are presumably the apocalyptic writings to which IV Ezra itself belongs.

The number 70 used in this connection may be purely symbolic, representing something that is comprehensive. Or, it may be more subtle in its reference than this. The word 'secret' (*swd*, pronounced sod), which occurs several times in this context, has in Hebrew a numerical value of 70 (s=60, w=6 and d=4), a factor which may have influenced the writer's use of this particular number. Be that as it may, Ezra the scribe who makes known the law of God is now presented as Ezra the scribe who, by divine revelation, is able to declare what has been and what will be, i.e. acting on behalf of Moses, he receives not only the canonical scriptures but also the apocalyptic books in a single revelation from God.

(d) A new revelation: apocalyptic and prophecy

The apocalyptists, then, believed themselves to be inheritors of the past, and sharers in God's revelation made known through his servant Moses. And that revelation, recorded in '24 books', contained not only the Torah, but the Prophets as well. As inheritors of the past, they were heirs of the prophets and sharers in their divine inspiration.

Closely related though they were, however, their perspective was different from that of prophetism, not least in its 'classical' form, in a number of significant respects:

For one thing, although they appealed to antiquity, they were not in fact particularly concerned about historical events as such in the way that the prophets were. Thus, in their writings there is hardly any reference, if any at all, to the deliverance from Egypt or the covenant at Sinai. They were concerned, it is true, with the political events of their own day, not least the tyranny of contemporary rulers, but the significance of such events was expressed, not in terms of contemporary politics, but rather in terms of a transcendent world which, though it impinged on this world of 'time and sense', went far beyond it for its ultimate meaning.

Secondly, in terms of inspiration, they related less to the classical form of prophecy than to its more primitive form – that of 'shamanic' prophetism which is reflected in large measure in mantic wisdom with its spirit-travel into the heavenly places. 'This extremely important aspect of apocalypticism', writes André Lacocque, 'is so far from cutting loose from its moorings in prophetism that it takes us back, on the contrary to (its) oldest forms, and even to a certain kind of shamanism; that is, to a stage in religion where the wise man and the oracular diviner were not distinguished, for both aspects were joined in the clairvoyant who *knows and forecasts* . . . If Daniel is "also among the prophets", he is nonetheless among the sages.'[2]

And thirdly, although prophet and apocalyptist alike believed they were recipients of divine revelation, their methods of making that revelation known were quite different.

The prophet, for the most part, delivered his message by means of the spoken word which might subsequently be put into writing either by himself or by his disciples or by future editors or redactors. The apocalyptist, on the other hand, remained concealed behind his message which he recorded in a book for the faithful among the people to read. God's command to the prophet was, 'Thou shalt speak unto them this word' (Jer. 13.12); his command to the apocalyptist was, 'What thou seest, write in a book' (Rev. 1.11). The prophet addressed his listeners with an authoritative, 'Thus saith the Lord' (Isa. 7.7, etc.); the apocalyptist, claiming a like authority, bade his readers, 'Receive this writing that thou mayest know how to preserve the books I shall deliver unto you' (Ass. of Moses 1.16).

This stress on the literary presentation of divine truth is characteristic of the whole apocalyptic school of thought.[3]

This is not to deny the apocalyptists' claim to inspiration or to invalidate the revelation received. There is an inspiration of the written word as there is of the spoken word, and revelation can be conveyed by pen as well as by tongue.

It is true that in the post-exilic period prophecy itself tended to become more literary in character. But even then the need was felt for such utterances and oracles to be closely associated with the 'living' voice of prophecy, and so it came often to be attached to the names and oracles of known prophets of the past. The method adopted by the apocalyptists, however, was altogether different. As we shall see more fully presently, they actually wrote what they had to say in the name of some revered hero of the past. The book thus produced – allegedly that of the ancient seer or prophet – was then passed down through succeeding generations, to be disclosed, apparently for the very first time, in the apocalyptist's own day.

2. METHODS AND MODES OF REVELATION

(a) Pseudonymous authorship

The phenomenon of pseudonymity was not peculiar to the Jewish writers, but was a fairly common practice throughout the Greek and Roman world. Where the Jewish apocalyptists were concerned, its use had at least two distinct advantages.

First, by tracing his revelation far back into antiquity and by claiming it for an ancient worthy highly respected for his wisdom and spiritual insight, the apocalyptic writer would win much greater prestige and authority for his book than he otherwise would have done had he written simply in his own name. What is more, in so doing he would be able to 'key into' the long and rich tradition with which the ancient hero's name was associated. Part of this would be handed down in literary form, but most would no doubt be received as oral tradition. Such tradition, as we saw in chapter 3, would readily gather round the names of great savants like Enoch, Abraham, Moses and

Ezra, to mention only a few, men whose reputation for wisdom and righteousness could not be gainsaid.

But the adoption of pseudonymity carried with it a second advantage. By means of this device, made possible by the literary character of apocalyptic, the writer was able to take his stand in the ancient past and from that vantage point to describe, albeit in cryptic terms, the course of 'future' generations right up to the writer's own day. The 'fulfilment' of his prophecies thus far would give added strength to his claim that the end was near and the messianic age was at hand. It mattered not apparently that the description of events up to the writer's own day were fairly clear but that after that point they became much more speculative and much more obscure.

But this phenomenon of *ex eventu* prophecy is of importance not simply as a means of 'forecasting' the future, but even more so of confirming a fundamental tenet of apocalyptic belief, namely, that the whole of history is predetermined by God, that the whole created universe is under his control and that he can be trusted to bring everything to its right conclusion (see chapter 5).

It might be thought – and indeed it has been thought – that the adoption of such a device was no more than a great charade whose intention was to deceive the reader and so gain acceptance for the book under false pretences. This, I believe, is much too facile a view and does not take fully enough into account the accepted literary conventions of the day or the peculiar 'psychology' of the writers themselves.

I have described pseudonymity, then, as a literary device which gave prestige to their recorded revelations, bolstered confidence in their 'predictions' and underlined the fact that all things are predetermined by the will of God and under his divine control. At the same time I have suggested that, in so doing, it was not their intention to deceive. But can such a claim be substantiated? How are we to explain otherwise this rather strange phenomenon on the part of these Jewish writers?

In a much earlier work[4] I argued in support of what has been described as 'a quasi-mystical union' between the apocalyptic writer and his mentor, and for this purpose made use of the two notions of 'corporate personality' (the group comprehends all the individuals belonging to it in a 'corporate unity' in such a way that there is an 'identity' between the individual and members of the group to which he belongs) and 'contemporaneity' (two separate events, because of the similarity of their 'psychological content' can be equated and seen as one). I recognize that these two notions have since then been strongly criticized and discredited.[5] I accept that criticism. Nevertheless, I believe that the basic contention remains and is not dependent on these two arguments. Let me re-state my position quite briefly without their help.

So widespread was the phenomenon of pseudonymity among the Jews and throughout the hellenistic world that it is difficult not to conclude that the writers, or many of them, were simply following an accepted and acceptable literary convention. But if this were so and if everyone recognized pseudonymity to be no more than a fiction, this would have robbed these writings of that very authority which the writers seem to have claimed for them.

It may well be, of course, that some readers believed that the books in question had actually been handed down from the ancient past. But it would surely be stretching credibility – and credulity – too far to imagine that the writers themselves accepted this in any literal sense. And yet there is a sense in which they might well have believed that the revelations they received and recorded had indeed come 'from ancient times'. The apocalyptic visionaries give the distinct impression that they were recipients of a genuine revelation of 'new things' culled, in fair measure, from scripture and from ancient tradition and so coming from bygone days. It may be that the solution to the problem is to be found, not in any desire to deceive, but in that sense of affinity or identity which the writer believed to exist between himself and the one in whose name he wrote.

In support of this, it would appear that the name of the pseudonymous author was not simply chosen at random. 'We must assume,' writes J. J. Collins, 'that the pseudonymous author was deliberately chosen because he was particularly appropriate for the real author's purpose. His name must have added to the effectiveness of the work, not only because of his authority, but also because of the values and ideas associated with it.'[6] Thus, the writer of I Enoch was a cosmopolitan like Enoch himself, the writer of Daniel shared with the

67

hero of the exile like circumstances and a like role as 'wise man', and the writer of IV Ezra reflected something of the narrow nationalism of that scribe of earlier days.

There was a recognizable affinity or identity between them, not so much in a 'quasi-mystical' sense as in the sense that they shared a common tradition and so a common experience of revelation and a common insight into the secret purposes of God. In their own visions and dreams they saw this patriarch or that prophet being introduced to the very mysteries to which they themselves had been introduced; together they were sharing a common experience and receiving a common revelation. In sharing with the other in this way the apocalyptic seer experienced a sense of identity with the hero of old, being introduced with him to mysteries hidden from the sight of other men. In that experience he was, in a deep sense, at one with the great man of old.

In describing the revelation received by the ancient seer, the apocalyptic visionaries (with the sole exception of the writer of Jubilees) expresses this identity by using the first and not the third person singular: 'I, Enoch, saw and beheld . . . ', 'I, Moses', 'I, Ezra' and so forth. The vision credited to the ancient was the apocalyptist's own vision and vice versa. An interesting illustration of this is perhaps to be found in I Enoch 1.2 where the writer begins by describing in the third person a vision experienced by Enoch; then, without warning, he slips over into the first person as if equating Enoch's experience with his own: '*Enoch*, a righteous man, whose eyes were opened by God saw a vision of the Holy One in the heavens, which the angels showed *me* and from them I heard everything.' A.R.C. Leaney makes this comment:

> The writer loses himself in the person whose special knowledge he claims to record. The identification is not merely a device . . . He believes that all knowledge has been already revealed to the patriarchs of old; he believes also with the same religious fervour that he has new and necessary knowledge to impart. A member of a people distinguished by a strong sense of the mutual inherence of the one and the many could in such circumstances feel without insincerity an identity with a representative person of his nation's past.[7]

The apocalyptists give the distinct impression that they are inheritors and not originators of the secret revelation they are now disclosing for the first time in their books. The reason for this may well be founded on the sincerely held belief that they stood in a distinct and continuous line of tradition going right back into early biblical times. The great worthies of the past, in whose names they wrote, stood at its beginning, and they, the apocalyptists, stood at its end. Together they shared in a common spiritual heritage and a common revelatory experience; and now, 'at the end of the days' to which the long tradition had pointed, they were privileged to share its secrets with 'the wise'. Seen in this light, the adoption of pseudonymity was no mere literary fiction but a reality with profound significance. The revelation they had received was their own, and yet it was not their own; it had been received from ancient times and ultimately from the one who, in his own revered person, exemplified the whole living tradition.

The patriarch or the prophet of old was the great exemplar, the fountain-head of all revealed knowledge. Just as all lawgiving throughout the ages could be credited to Moses the fountainhead of all lawgiving, and all psalmody to David the fountainhead of all song, and all wisdom to Solomon the fountainhead of all wisdom, so all revealed truth, of whatever age and whatever kind, could be credited to the ancient worthy who was the spring and source of all revelation. The revelation vouchsafed to the apocalyptist was not his own but Enoch's or Moses' or Ezra's according to the particular tradition in which he stood.

For some of the apocalyptic writers, no doubt, the adoption of pseudonymity was little more than the following out of a literary convention. But for others it represented a profound understanding of the origin and medium of divine disclosure. In either case the charge of deception cannot stand. On the contrary, pseudonymous authorship is an honest medium in revealing the hidden mysteries of God. Nor indeed is it simply a device; it is a declaration that the truth revealed of old has at last reached its consummation.

(b) Symbolic in language

Another feature of this literature which is an easily recognizable part of the apocalyptist's stock-in-trade was his use of symbolic language. Sometimes it is the fruit of a fertile imagination; at other times it is a legacy from the distant past, reflecting perhaps the colourful worship of Solomon's Temple or the mythology of ancient civilizations. Sometimes the symbolic pictures presented are easy to understand; at other times they are obscure in the extreme or else seem to have no meaning at all, but simply belong to a stereotyped mechanism handed down from the past. Such symbolic language shows kaleidoscopic variations.

Animals. One is the use of animal figures of all kinds to symbolize men and nations, to be found especially in the Enoch traditions, though there is no consistency of usage. The bull, for example, is a symbol of the patriarchs, though it may be used of the Messiah and the members of his Kingdom. The righteous who come after the patriarchs are sheep or lambs and at one point the Messiah is changed from a bull to a lamb! Judas Maccabeus is a ram or a ram's horn. The twelve tribes are twelve harts which become sheep and then bulls. The Gentiles are described under the figure of wild animals – lions, tigers, wolves, dogs, hyenas, wild boars, foxes, squirrels, swine, falcons, vultures, kites, eagles and ravens. The lion represents the tribe of Judah and also symbolizes the Messiah.

Men and stars. Just as men and nations are symbolized by animals, so good angels are symbolized by men and fallen angels by stars. The 'men' are sometimes said to be dressed in 'white garments'; these represent their 'spiritual bodies' as they do the resurrection bodies of the righteous. The fallen angels are falling stars. At times the symbolism runs riot as when these stars become bulls which sire elephants, camels and asses representing three kinds of giants!

Mythological creatures. Some of the mythological language describes monsters of different kinds to be found already in the Old Testament, such as the Dragon, Leviathan, Behemoth and the Serpent. The exact identification of such monsters, as we have seen, varies from book to book, but always they indicate that which is evil and at enmity against God. Sometimes they are given an eschatological setting and are in conflict with the Messiah. On God's Great Day they will be slain and devoured as food.

The Messianic Banquet. This last reference calls to mind yet another symbol, that of the Messianic Banquet to be celebrated in the Messianic Age to which allusion is made in the Qumran texts, in the rabbinical literature and, of course, in the New Testament itself.

Numbers. One other symbol worthy of note is that of number. Frequent use is made, for example, of the numbers 3, 4, 10 and 12 or multiples of them. We have already noted the symbolic significance of 70. We note also the use of 7 in the New Testament Apocalypse where it appears no fewer than 54 times. Numbers are of supreme importance in their interpretation of prophecy, for example, and especially in their calculation of the End-time. They form an integral part of the schematization of history which had such a fascination for these writers which enabled them to calculate the time of that Great Day of which the prophets had spoken when the mysteries of God would be finally and fully revealed.

Meantime the apocalyptists had special insight into these mysteries through divine revelation. We look now at the means by which such revelation was believed to be received.

3. MEDIA OF REVELATION

An apocalypse is essentially a revelation or a record of a revelation, made known, as we shall see, by certain fairly stereotyped means and disclosing certain professed 'secrets' which reveal the ways of God with the world and with those who dwell in it. Or, to put it another way, it is a revelation marked by certain characteristics which relate first to the manner of its reception and communication and second to the nature of its contents and message. In subsequent chapters we shall look at the second of these. At this point we shall consider the first – the means by which the revelation was believed to be given and the 'devices' or 'techniques' employed.

(a) Dream-visions

The forms the revelation takes are many and varied, but undoubtedly most frequent use is made of the symbolic dream-vision which assumes throughout these writings a fairly distinctive pattern. A description is given of the circumstances or particular occasion leading up to the revelation and this is followed by a description of the dream or vision itself; reference is then made to the reaction of the recipient who requests an interpretation of what he has seen; this interpretation is usually given by an angel; the conclusion of the episode takes various forms in keeping with the circumstances with which the account began. It is clear from similar occurrences in non-Jewish writings of the period that such an outline followed a recognized conventional pattern which, though it allowed for many variations, was a commonly accepted device employed fairly widely throughout the Near East.

There are connections between this form of revelation and that of, say, the biblical tradition, particularly as this finds expression in the visions of Zechariah with their accompanying angelic interpretation. But it is clear that there is no single line of tradition stretching back into the past. The substance of the vision is culled from many sources and probably owes much to that mantic wisdom to which reference has already been made. The result is a very different 'product' from that of, say, Amos or Jeremiah. The influence of Ezekiel is much more evident, as in the Book of Daniel; but the apocalyptic writers as a whole are open to the influence of varied traditions, biblical and non-biblical alike, and at the same time reveal no small creative imagination of their own.

So different indeed are many of these visions from those in the biblical tradition that they generally make little or no sense as they stand and require superhuman interpretation. This, as just noted and as we shall see more fully later, is normally given by an angel or archangel. On those occasions when Daniel is called upon to give the interpretation of someone else's dream, he goes out of his way to emphasize that such interpretation is dependent, not on any wisdom he may possess, but solely on the wisdom of God who alone can reveal such mysteries. The nature of the interpretation may vary from one situation to another, but for the most part it is allegorical in character; what is seen in the dream or vision represents something else: the statue in Daniel or the metals from which it is made or the four beasts and the eagle that emerge from the sea – all these and many more convey a message from beyond, a message that is to be understood, for example, in terms of the kings and kingdoms of this world.

Such visions, with their accompanying interpretations, moreover, do not simply rise of their own accord out of the apocalyptist's fertile imagination. They do not just come, they are sent by God as his chosen vehicle of revelation. The distinction that moderns make between 'subjective' and 'objective' experiences would not have entered into his mind at all and would have made no sense if they did. The dreams and visions, together with their interpretations, are 'objective' revelations which are given and received. They are given by God who is the source of divine wisdom, and they are received by those who are open to him and ready to respond with an upright and righteous life. It is not by accident that men like Enoch, Daniel, Abraham, Moses and Ezra are again and again introduced to the reader as 'righteous' and 'wise' in the eyes of God, for it is to such as these that God is pleased to make known the mysteries of heaven and the secrets of his creation.

Here, then, in dreams and visions the apocalyptist has found a graphic technique whereby he is able to introduce his readers to those 'mysteries' that so intrigue him and which, he believes, uncover the very wisdom of God himself. And yet there are indications that what we have here may be much more than simply a literary device or the carrying out of a literary convention and that behind what appears to be a 'literary fiction', as it were, we are to detect genuine visionary experience on the part of some at least of the apocalyptic writers. This is suggested by a number of factors which may point in this direction:

Parallels in related writings and cultures. Thomas J. Sappington helpfully suggests parallels in related writings and cultures which give supporting evidence for the presence here of visionary-experience.[8] A number of the Old Testament prophets, for example, refer to ecstatic vision or audition as the vehicle of the oracle they now record. Since the apocalyptic writers (or a number of them at least) appear to have shared the 'prophetic consciousness' and even express themselves in the form of older prophecy, it would not be at all surprising if this continuity between prophet and apocalyptist were to express itself in similar visionary experience.

Again, there are close connections, as we have seen, between Jewish apocalyptic and mantic wisdom whose practitioners based their written words on actual revelatory experience. It is a fair assumption, particularly when backed up by other similar evidence, that behind a number of the apocalyptic books there may well have been visionary experience of somewhat the same kind. This finds support in the later Merkabah mysticism, for which Jewish apocalyptic offered a precedent, which gives plentiful evidence of mystical experience.

And, of course, there is the evidence of the New Testament itself, not only in Paul's letters (cf. II Cor. 12.1–9), but even more so in the Book of Revelation which shares with Jewish apocalyptic something of that same mystical experience.

And finally, there is ample evidence of parallels with the visionary experience expressed in other cultures and societies of that time. Here the work of Susan Niditch[9] is of particular value, demonstrating as it does parallels with shamans, ecstatics and mystics of various kinds. Such parallels, especially when taken together, add up to a strong case for the contention that what we have in Jewish apocalyptic is not just a literary convention but the reflection of genuine visionary and mystical experience.

The language used. Another contributory factor pointing in the same direction is the evidence of the language used to describe the dream or vision which is so graphic and so true to life as to suggest that it reflects the apocalyptist's own dream- or trance-like experience. The recipient, we are told, is agitated beyond measure (Dan. 7.28; cf. II Enoch 6.36f.); he is in a state of utter bewilderment (II Enoch 10.27); so overwhelmed is he that he is quite incapable of expressing himself adequately or he may even be struck dumb (II Enoch 10.15) or else lose consciousness altogether (II Enoch 8.18). Such descriptions are so true to experience that it is again difficult to see in them simply an expression of literary convention.

Preparations made. This impression is further strengthened when we read of the preparations made by the apocalyptist in readiness for the reception of the dream or vision. He gives himself over to a long period of prayer (Dan. 2.18f.; IV Ezra 5.13; 6.31, 35; 9.23–28, etc.)

and fasting (Dan. 10.3; IV Ezra 5.13; II Bar. 9.2, etc.); or he confines himself to a strict diet (Dan. 10.2f.; IV Ezra 9.23 ff.; II Bar. 29.5, 8, etc); or, as in the case of Ezra, he drinks a special potion which fills him with the spirit of wisdom and spiritual insight (IV Ezra 14.38ff.). Revelations are not dependent on such preparations, but they are obviously conducive to their reception as are, for example, special places and particular times. In this latter connection the time of sleep or the semi-somnolent state are special occasions for dreams and visions and so of revelation.

Such references, of course, may signify no more than a traditional, stereotyped pattern; but the fact remains that this is how the apocalyptist thought a revelation might most readily come, and so there is at least an *a priori* argument that such descriptions reflect actual experience. The experience credited to the ancient seer, would then be a reflection of the apocalyptist's own.

(b) Otherworldly journeys

This conclusion finds corroboration in a particular form of vision in which the ancient seer is taken on an exciting journey through the heavens or to the ends of the earth. We have already noted examples of this in I Enoch 1–37 and 37–71, II Enoch, the Testament of Levi 2–5, the Apocalypse of Abraham, the Testament of Abraham and the Apocalypse of Zephaniah (see chapter 3). Once more there are close similarities with the practices and beliefs of other Near Eastern cultures, particularly those of mantic wisdom where the shaman is said to undergo the same experience.

There is no actual precedent for such journeys in the Old Testament records, but we recall in this connection how the prophet takes his place in the heavenly council where he receives God's word to deliver to the people (Jer. 23.18; cf. I Kings 22). There are biblical accounts of permanent ascents as in the cases of Enoch and Elijah who were taken up into heaven, to be seen no more, and in Jewish tradition the same thing is said of Moses (cf. the Assumption of Moses). In the apocalyptic books, however, the journeys made by the ancient seer are of a temporary character. Once the revelation has been given and received, he returns to earth to make known to 'the wise' what he has seen and heard.

75

All revelation is from heaven where wisdom dwells. Sometimes it is sent down by God to earth and is made known to the seer in dream or vision; at other times it awaits him in heaven itself where it is disclosed in all its glory and wonder. Typical of such a journey is that described in I Enoch 14.8: 'And behold, I saw the clouds: and they were calling me in a vision, and the fogs were calling me; and the course of the stars and the lightnings were rushing me and . . . the winds were causing me to fly and rushing me high up into heaven.' There he is surrounded by myriads of angels (I En. 71.8) and sees 'the Great Glory' seated upon his throne (I En. 14.20), or else he travels to the ends of the earth where he is introduced to the mysteries of the universe (I En. 71.4): he sees where the winds are stored and where the rain and hail and snow are kept in readiness for the winter's storms (I En. 41–44). From his vantage point he is able to view the whole of history (I En. 85.1ff.) from its beginning to its end and is shown clearly how, despite tragedies and persecutions, everything works out perfectly in the end. Or else, his journey takes him to the realm of the departed where he sees the bliss of the righteous and the fate of the wicked (I En. 22). Sometimes what he sees is breathtaking and glorious; at other times it is more like a nightmare. His account is often dressed in symbolic language, coloured through and through with mythological imagery depicting sacred mountains, fiery angels and monstrous beasts (I En. 60.7f.).

More often than not the translation envisaged is that of the spirit; occasionally it is in bodily form as in the Testament of Abraham where it is said: 'Michael . . . caught up Abraham in the body upon a cloud' (8.3B). Elsewhere the 'means of transport' is said to be 'the right wing of a pigeon' (Apoc. of Abr. 15) or angels' wings (II En. 3.1).

The heavenly journey often takes the form of a guided tour as in the Astronomical Book of Enoch, the Similitudes of Enoch and the Testament of Abraham. In the Enoch books the seer is taken to the ends of the earth and shown the wonders of creation; and in the Testament of Abraham he is conveyed around in a chariot 'over all the earth' (10.1A). At other times the journey takes him through a numbered series of heavens to the very throne of God himself. In the earlier books the number of heavens is thought to be three (as in the Testament of Levi 2–5), but in later books it is seven. At each stage fresh revelations are given which find their blinding climax in the glory of God.

The seer in his journeys does not travel alone. He is accompanied sometimes by a host of angels and at other times by a single angelic guide.

(c) Mediation of angels

This brings us to yet another technique, found already in the Old Testament, but assuming much larger proportions during the intertestamental years – the mediatorial function of angels who appear in profusion in book after book and become a marked feature of this whole literature.

Angels are divine messengers who shuttle back and forth between heaven and earth, between God and men, carrying men's prayers to God and God's response to men – celestial postmen who act promptly, as celestial postmen should! Sometimes, however, they are delayed through no fault of their own as in the case of Gabriel who, in response to Daniel's prayer, was held up for no less than three weeks (Dan. 10.12f.), having been waylaid, we are told, by the guardian angel of Persia, but rescued from his clutches by Israel's guardian angel Michael.

But more common in these writings is their function as celestial guides or celestial interpreters. It is an angelic attendant, for example, who escorts Enoch round the heavenly galleries (I En. 72–82) and shows him the vaults where the natural elements are stored (I En. 76). But more important than this, it is the angels or archangels who have the responsibility of revealing to the privileged few the secrets of earth and heaven. These 'secrets' are inscribed in 'the books of the holy ones', i.e. of the angels (I En. 103.2; 108.2), books which they have not only recorded but also studied and by means of which they are able to disclose to men the mysteries of the universe. Enoch, we are told, spent six jubilees of years with the angels of God who 'showed him everything which is on earth and in the heavens, the rule of the sun, and he wrote down everything' (Jub. 4.21). By such means they were able to reveal the history of bygone ages as well as the time ahead which until now had, as it were, been kept 'under wraps'. All these things showed – as did all the other 'devices' used in these writings –

that the end was near; the ultimate fulfilment of all the ages was close at hand.

(d) Secret books

Reference has been made to the account given in IV Ezra 14 of how Ezra the scribe was bidden by God to re-write the 24 (canonical) books and the 70 (secret/apocalyptic) books which, it is indicated, had previously been written by Moses but had subsequently been destroyed by fire. Such an account reminds us that this notion of secret books of great antiquity, passed on through generation after generation – or even descending from heaven itself – was a fairly common one among the Greeks and was adopted by the Jewish apocalyptic writers as eminently suitable for their purpose. It expressed in a graphic way their conviction that the books they were now writing were not simply their own creation; they were the deposit of a long tradition which they themselves had inherited and were now disclosing to those among the people who were wise enough to understand.

As we have seen, there are several strands of tradition which find expression in the varied apocalyptic writings. In each of them this particular technique is used to good effect. We find it reflected in the Book of Daniel, for example, where Daniel, having received revelations from God, is bidden to 'shut up the words and seal the book' (12.9; cf. Rev. 10.4) – a book which eventually will be opened and read at the appointed time of 'the end', which most appropriately corresponds to the time of the apocalyptic writer himself during the reign of the Syrian tyrant, Antiochus Epiphanes!

Another strand of tradition is that associated with the name of Moses. In the Book of Jubilees, for example, Moses is bidden to write down all that he has seen in the revelation vouchsafed to him: 'Write down for yourself all the matters which I shall make known to you on this mountain: what was in the beginning and what will be at the end . . . until I shall descend and dwell with them in all the ages of eternity' (1.26). But not only has he to record these things; he has also to preserve them and pass them on to his descendants and they to theirs until the last time when their contents will at last be disclosed. This is spelt out clearly in the Testament of Moses, where Moses instructs his successor Joshua in these words: 'Take this writing so that later you will remember how to preserve the books which I shall entrust to you. You shall arrange them, anoint them with cedar (oil) and deposit them in earthenware jars in the place which God has chosen from the beginning of the creation of the world' (1.16f.).

In other traditions such books are linked with other great names from the past, especially with that of Enoch. According to the Book of Jubilees, for example, Enoch is bidden to record in a book the revelation he has received and then to pass it on, first to Noah and then through him to succeeding generations: 'Thus, Enoch the father of your father, commanded Methuselah his son, and Methuselah (commanded) Lamech his son. And Lamech commanded me (Noah) everything which his fathers commanded him. And I am commanding you, my sons, just as Enoch commanded his son in the first jubilee' (7.38f.). Noah, we are told, then passed on what he had received in a book to his son Shem (10.14) who in turn passed on its secrets to Abraham who, according to Jewish tradition, studied in the school of Shem, and then through Isaac and Jacob and from there into the hands of Levi (45.16) with whose descendants, it is said, they remain 'until this day' – no doubt indicating that the author of Jubilees was himself a priest and a descendant of Levi.

This same Enoch tradition is elaborated still further elsewhere. In Jubilees 4.21, we recall, we are told that 'he was with the angels of God six jubilees of years. And they showed him everything that is on earth and in the heavens . . . and he wrote everything down' (cf. also I Enoch 106.13). In another branch of the tradition, represented this time by the Second Book of Enoch, he is bidden once more to write down what he has seen and heard. He does so and fills no fewer than 366 volumes (II En. 23.6)! These he has to take back with him from heaven to earth as an encouragement to those who will survive in the last days (ch. 35).

The story is continued with reference to Abraham in Jubilees 21.10 where that patriarch refers to what he has found written in 'the books of my forefathers and in the words of Enoch and in the words of Noah'. Elsewhere in the same book we are told that he 'took his father's books – and they were written in Hebrew – and he copied them . . . and he studied them in the six months of rain' (12.15–27).

To sum up, then. The task of passing on the ancient tradition, going right back to the great man of old in whose name the apocalyptist writes and carrying with it his authority, has at last been faithfully discharged. The very fact that the book is now being published is a sure sign that the Great Day of the Lord is at hand.

(e) Meditation on scripture

One other technique that most likely reflects the apocalyptist's own experience is that of meditation on scripture. A good example of this is to be found in Dan. 9.24ff. where the ancient hero, Daniel himself, in his reading of scripture, is greatly puzzled by the reference in Jer. 25.11–12 to the 70 years during which Israel would remain in captivity. The puzzlement credited to Daniel no doubt reflects that of the apocalyptic writer himself in the time of Antiochus Epiphanes around the year 165 BC. This was a passage that he himself had studied and found so bewildering. By his time the 70 years had long since passed and deliverance had not yet come. What was the meaning of it? The answer given by the man Daniel in the book expresses the deeply felt conviction of the writer himself, namely that by those '70 years' was meant '70 weeks of years', i.e. 490 years, which would bring the period of waiting down to the apocalyptic writer's own day and would confirm him in his belief that the time of persecution under Antiochus would soon be over and God's final deliverance of his people would at last have come. It may be that this interpretation was influenced by his reading such passages as II Chron. 36.21 and Lev. 26.34f. which state that during the time that Israel lay desolate 'she kept sabbaths to fulfil three score and ten years', i.e. the '70 years' are to be interpreted as '70 sabbaths of years' or '70 heptads of years', i.e. '490 years' in all. The meditation and interpretation of scripture given by the man Daniel is a direct reflection of the conviction of the actual writer as he himself wrestles with the promises of God made known through the prophet. Literary device it may be, but it is a powerful technique in conveying to the reader the writer's deep conviction that the word of God will not be broken and that the fulfilment of his promise is near at hand.

The fulfilment of ancient prophecy, the writer believes, will find its realization in his own generation. The 'technique' he uses to convey his deeply-felt conviction is a counterpart of his use of that pseudonymity by which he is able to 'identify' himself with the seer of old. The foretelling of the prophet yesterday is the forthtelling of the apocalyptist today.

V

Divine Secrets Revealed

'There is a God in heaven', says Daniel, 'who reveals secrets' (Dan. 2.28). The apocalyptic books as a whole claim, as we have seen, to be revelations or disclosures of divine secrets, concealed in heaven and so hidden from human eyes, but made known by God to certain illustrious men of by-gone days who subsequently recorded them in secret books for the encouragement of 'the wise' in future years and for the instruction of 'the many' that they in turn might also become wise. In the Book of Daniel alone the word 'secret' or 'mystery' (Aramaic, *raz*; Greek, *mysterion*) occurs no fewer than nine times and finds frequent mention in the Qumran texts together with the word *swd* (see p. 63), signifying a divine mystery whose interpretation is granted to a select few.

But what exactly were these mysteries, made known through visions and dreams and by the agency of angels? It is clear that they were extremely diverse in both range and content. They concerned 'knowledge and understanding of all kinds of literature and learning' (Dan. 1.20); they embraced not only matters relating to earthly experience, but 'all the secret things of heaven and the future things' as well (I En. 52.1). Indeed, so diverse were they that they could be said to include 'all things of God' (III Bar. 1.4, Greek text). Broadly speaking, however, it may be said they were divine revelations concerning three areas about which there was much speculation: cosmology, history and eschatology.

I. COSMOLOGY

Several 'lists of revealed things'[1] are given throughout these writings which illustrate still further the great variety of 'secrets' stored up on earth and in heaven for those privileged to see them for themselves. Most are made known, as we have observed, as a result of journeys made in vision by the ancient seer through heaven itself. Examples of these are to be found in I Enoch 41.1–7; 43.1–2; 60.11–22; II Enoch 23.1; 40.1–13; II Baruch 59.5–11 and *Liber Antiquitatum Biblicarum* 19.10. They contain a wide range of disclosed 'mysteries' and represent a great variety of topics, but in large part they are cosmological in character, revealing to the ancient seer the mysteries of earth and heaven.

(a) The created world

In common with others of their generation, the apocalyptic writers were keenly interested not only in the creation of the earth as recorded in the early chapters of Genesis, but also in the creation of the entire cosmos with its heavenly bodies and its cosmic forces so difficult to distinguish from each other. The sun, the moon, the planets and the stars, together with all the natural elements, were mysteries whose secrets had been made known by divine revelation – the courses they followed, their place within the created universe, the storehouses where they were kept, the purpose of their movements, their function in the eternal purpose of God and so forth.

The writer of the Wisdom of Solomon indicates Judaism's widespread interest in such matters when he speaks of 'what is secret and what is manifest' in terms of 'the structure of the world and the activity of the elements . . . the alternations of the solstices and the changes of the seasons, the cycles of the year and the constellations of the stars' (7.17ff.). These and their like are all the gift of divine wisdom (7.21f.). The same sentiment is echoed by Ben Sira who asserts that 'many things greater than these lie hidden, for we have seen but few of his works' (43.32).

There is relatively little interest shown throughout the apocalyptic writings in geographical features as such, although Jubilees 2.2ff. does give a detailed account of the creation of the world in six days and sets out the work of creation in three tiers – the heavens where God dwells with his holy angels, the earth with its great oceans and its division into three continents, and 'the abysses and the darkness' beneath the earth.

But such observations of 'the seen' are of much less importance than the vision of 'the unseen'. Cosmogony merged into cosmology and astronomy became hardly distinguishable from astrology. More significant than the actual work of creation were the order and purpose that lay behind creation. The stars and other heavenly bodies were more than objects in the sky; they represented cosmic powers that influenced men's destiny. God was a God of order, as shown in his governance of the universe and in his control of the seasons. The secrets of that order and that governance had to be understood if his will was to be done and his commands obeyed.

Such 'mysteries' are the subject of much speculation in book after book, as in I Enoch and II Baruch, and to a lesser extent in the Qumran texts. Some of this cosmic speculation, as we have already observed, has to do with the calendar and the fixing of dates for the religious festivals over which meticulous care had to be taken. The so-called Book of the Heavenly Luminaries, for example, contained in I Enoch 72–82, deals specifically with laws relating to the heavenly bodies and their bearing on calendrical calculations. Reference is made there and elsewhere to the signs of the Zodiac which are in the control of the angels and are believed to determine the destinies of men and nations. Such thinking influenced even strict Jews like those of the Qumran sect among whose writings there has been found an astrological cryptic document referring to a man born under the sign of Taurus the Bull.

(b) The throne of God

In later times attention came to be focussed on two mystical doctrines which played an important part in Jewish theological and metaphysical debate: the *Ma'aseh bereshith*, meaning 'the work (of God) in the beginning', based on the creation narrative in Genesis 1, and the *Merkabah*, meaning 'chariot', based largely on the description of the chariot-throne of God described in Ezekiel 1 – two doctrines which, at an early stage in their development, are reflected in the apocalyptic writings. So much 'dangerous speculation' came to be associated with their exposition that in due course the rabbis felt obliged to utter a warning 'not to expound the chapter of Genesis before more than one hearer nor that of the heavenly chariot to any but a man of wisdom and profound understanding' (*Hagigah* 2.1).

We have seen the significant part played by the doctrine of creation in the apocalyptic writings; we note also frequent reference to the chariot-throne theme in which the seer is ushered into the glorious presence of the Most High God either in a vision (cf. Dan. 7) or as the climax of a heavenly journey (cf. I En. 14, 60, 71; Test. of Levi 5; II En. 20–21; Apoc. of Abraham 18).

The earliest reference to the Merkabah in our literature is in I Enoch 14 where the seer describes his ascent through the heavens until at last he is confronted by the glorious throne of God: 'Behold, in the vision . . . I approached a wall which was built of white marble and surrounded by tongues of fire . . . And behold there was an opening before me (and) a second house which is greater than the former, and everything was built with tongues of fire . . . As for the floor, it was fire and above it was lightning and the path of the stars; and as for the ceiling it was flaming fire. And I observed and saw inside it a lofty throne – its appearance was like crystal and its wheels like the shining sun . . . and from beneath the throne were issuing streams of flaming fire. It was difficult to look at it. And the Great Glory was sitting upon it . . . The flaming fire was round about him, and a great fire stood before him. No one could come near unto him among those that surrounded the tens of millions that stood before him' (I En. 14.8–22).

Such a passage recalls the vivid description in the Book of Revelation of the throne of God which the seer was privileged to behold through an open door in heaven: 'He who sat there appeared like jasper and cornelian, and round the throne was a rainbow that looked like emerald' (4.3); or the reference to the 'great white throne' from which God would at the last judge all the world (20.11). In the Similitudes of Enoch a somewhat fuller description is given of this glorious God; strange and obscure names are given to him and to the holy angels who surround his throne, special power being acquired by those who have knowledge of their secret meaning, especially when used in oaths.

Visions of this kind are not confined to I Enoch or indeed to the

Enoch tradition as reflected, for example, in the Slavonic Enoch. In the Testament of Levi 3.8, the Apocalypse of Zephaniah 8.2–4 and the Apocalypse of Abraham 17.8–21 much more is said not only about the glory of God and his majestic throne, but also about the angel-hosts who surround that throne and wait upon him day and night. Much speculation is expressed in the writers' description and identification of them as in the Similitudes of Enoch were 'the living creatures' and even the hubs of Ezekiel's chariot are transformed into angels 'who sleep not and guard the throne of his glory' (I En. 71.7; cf. 61.10).

Here, then, we have a picture of a wholly transcendent God, whose great glory is blinding in its magnificence and whose presence is portrayed in flames of fire. He is the inaccessible God, guarded by millions upon millions of angels, entry into whose presence is granted only by special decree and whose face is to be seen only by those chosen to behold him by divine revelation. Enoch, the righteous, was one of these and with him the other privileged few. The mysteries of God are to be found not only in creation, but also in the very being of God himself.

2. HISTORY

(a) The God of history

It is part of the genius of the apocalyptic visionaries that they were able to see, perhaps more clearly than many who had gone before them, that the great God, transcendent in the heavens and seated on his glorious throne, was nevertheless deeply involved in the history of his people and indeed in the history of the whole human race. The 'wholly other', who in the beginning had created the heavens and the earth and had kept the cosmos in his control, was the same God who created kings and kingdoms and controlled their rise and fall.

It has often been argued that the apocalyptists were not interested in history as such, except in so far as it led up to 'the End'. This, however, needs some qualification in the light of the evidence of the apocalyptic books themselves with their frequent reviews of world history and their equally frequent allusions to contemporary events, all of which point to the fact that they did indeed take history seriously and were interested in it for its own sake. The God of creation was to them the God of history; the transcendent God was the immanent God; the detached God was the involved God; the God far away was the God near at hand. To them, the movements of world events were as much God's concern as the movements of the sun, the moon and the stars; historical events were of one piece with cosmic events. The one reflected – and replicated – the other. The world of earthly powers was inextricably bound up with the world of earthly powers; angels mingled with men; cosmic forces stood shoulder to shoulder with military might; celestial phenomena appeared as terrestrial signs.

If the 'vertical' apocalypses, with their otherworldly journeys, give the one emphasis, the 'horizontal' apocalypses, with their panoramic views of world history, give the other. And yet, both emphases are equally valid and are indeed complementary. Together they express the apocalyptists' belief that the God who in the beginning created the universe is the same God who now and always is in total charge of the affairs of men.

(b) The unity of history

Corresponding to the wholeness of creation, moreover, there was a wholeness of history both of which spoke of the wholeness of God.[2] Like the prophets before them, the apocalyptists were able to see history, not just in terms of contemporary event, but in terms also of a unity that embraced all peoples and all times. But unlike the prophets, they were able to interpret these things *sub specie aeternitatis*, from the stand-point of eternity, and so were able in all the confusions of history and in all its trials and persecutions, to see both a purpose and a goal. Contemporary experience was to be seen, not in isolation, but as part of that wholeness of human history which declared, on the authority of God himself, that despite all appearances to the contrary he was in complete control. The people might be living in a time of great crisis; things might be going from bad to worse; the whole world-order might seem 'beyond redemption'; events might be moving inexorably to their fateful conclusion; rulers like Alexander and tyrants like Antiochus might claim universal sway and exhibit complete sovereignty over their subjects. But the 'mystery' now disclosed to these visionaries was that the God who reigned in glory 'above' was the same God who reigned in power 'below'. The sovereign claims of tyrants were as nothing compared with the sovereign rule of God who not only 'changes times and seasons' but 'removes kings and sets them up' as well (Dan. 2.21). Kings and kingdoms, however powerful and however tyrannical, were under his authority and in his control. The Almighty had a plan for creation and for the whole human race – past, present and future – which would inevitably and speedily be fulfilled.

(c) 'Predicting' the past

This sense of belonging to the wholeness of history which is in God's control is further strengthened by the adoption of *ex eventu* prophecy, i.e. prophecy in which the events of the past are 'predicted' as if they were still to come, a concept which, as we have seen, lies behind the adoption of pseudonymous authorship. It occurs in only one of the 'otherworldly' apocalypses, the Apocalypse of Abraham, where the patriarch in his heavenly journey is shown a panoramic view of the earth, its inhabitants and its history, fast drawing to its close. It is a prominent feature, however, in all the 'historical' apocalypses. Thus, in Daniel 2.31ff. the hero of the exile 'foretells' the demise of four great 'future' empires and their rulers as depicted in Nebuchadnezzar's dream of a statue in four parts which is crushed and replaced by a stone representing the Kingdom of God, and similarly in 7.1–14 where four beasts that rise out of the sea, also signifying kings and kingdoms, meet with a similar fate. Sovereign states come under judgment by the sovereign Lord. The same lesson is taught in I Enoch 85ff. where the time-span extends from creation to the writer's own day, whilst the Apocalypse of Weeks takes us from the time of Enoch to the post-exilic period. Other reviews are presented in the so-called 'eagle-vision' in IV Ezra 11–12 and in the vision of the black and clear waters in II Baruch 53–74 which gives an outline of world history from the time of Adam to the dawning of the new age.

By so 'predicting' history with its rise and fall of nations, the writer gave greater credence to his book and in particular to the prophecies he was making concerning 'the End' itself. If what he said about the passing generations was seen to be accurate, could not the same be said of his predictions concerning the time to come? Christopher

Rowland puts the matter pictorially by likening the apocalyptic view of history to 'a play with many scenes which have been written but not all acted out on stage . . . The apocalyptic seer is privileged to have a total view of the play, including that which is still to be actualized on the stage of history.'[3] They were able, as it were, to take in the whole of history at a glance and to declare with confidence its ultimate meaning in terms of the unified purpose of God.

As recipients of such a secret, these men of fear became men of faith, able to see within history, through history and beyond history the working out of God's triumphant purpose. They believed that 'man's extremity was God's opportunity'. This 'extremity' would signal 'the End' when the Kingdom of God would replace the kingdoms of this world and he would reign for ever.

(d) History systematized and predetermined

But in their use of *ex eventu* prophecy the apocalyptists went further still. Not only did they 'predict' the great sweep of past events, they broke history up, as it were, into pre-determined periods or epochs in such a way that it was possible to recognize much more precisely the course of events and, more importantly, to identify the end of the process and the coming of God's promised Kingdom. In so doing, they went much further than the prophets and reflected a notion of history common within the hellenistic culture of their own time which owed much, it would seem, to the influence of Persian thought, where clear parallels are to be found of the division of history into four, or seven or ten or twelve distinct parts.

Many different schemes, corresponding to these divisions, are recorded in the apocalyptic books, indicating a variety of well-defined traditions with different divisions and different durations. In each case they are set out with mathematical precision, underlining still further both the unity of history and the complete control of God over its movements, who has determined from the beginning not only the course of its events but their climax as well.

Sometimes, as in Daniel 11, the schematization is limited to a relatively short period of time or to the reign of a single king whose years are 'predicted' precisely and whose demise is assuredly declared. More often than not, however, the seer's vision sweeps over vast areas of time, 'predicting' whole generations, identifying the rise and fall of empires and confirming that 'the End' is near. Thus, the writer of Daniel, as we have seen, divides up history, from the time of the Exile onwards, into seventy 'weeks of years' on the basis of Jeremiah's prophecy. These in turn are divided into three periods of seven 'weeks', sixty-two 'weeks' and one 'week' after which the End will come. In I Enoch 1–36 the period from the Flood to the Final Judgment is given as seventy 'generations' and in I Enoch 83–90 history is ruled over by seventy angelic 'shepherds' who are set over the nations of the earth and whose reigns are divided in turn into four ages ruled over by twelve, twenty-three, twenty-three and twelve 'shepherds'. Such a four-fold division is familiar to us from our reading of the Book of Daniel with its four-metal statue (Dan. 2) and its four fearsome beasts rising out of the sea (Dan. 7.3) and reflects the commonly accepted classification of world history into Gold, Silver, Bronze and Iron Ages.

Reference is made in IV Ezra 14.5 to a secret tradition associated with the name of Moses regarding great crises of world history. This is spelt out further in Jubilees and the Assumption of Moses where the jubilee is used as a measurement, whilst in the Enoch Apocalypse of Weeks history is divided into ten 'weeks', seven of which have already passed. In yet other books the division is made into twelve parts: in the Testament of Abraham, for example, the world's duration of seven thousand years is divided into 'twelve hours of the day', each 'hour' representing a hundred years; so too in II Baruch where the waters, symbolizing periods of world history, are poured out on the earth twelve times (53.6), and in IV Ezra where it is stated that only two and a half of the twelve parts still remain.

By such means as these the apocalyptists build up a schematized pattern of history which, given the fiction of 'prediction' here adopted, proves irrefutably that history both in whole and in its several parts has been predetermined by the sovereign will of God. By the use of what we might call 'slide-rule (or computerized!) theology' they are able to identify where they themselves now stand in the developing course of events and to ascertain that they in fact have come very near to the culmination of the whole historical process. It is small wonder that their critics called them rather derisively 'calculators of the end'.

Their juggling with numbers might seem to us artificial and question-begging in the extreme, but there can be little doubt that by this means they brought great assurance to their readers and found great consolation in it themselves. Nothing that the most powerful ruler could do could in any way alter the fact that God had determined all things from the beginning and would bring them to their successful conclusion. The years were 'numbered' – in more ways than one! God's people stood now on the very brink of the coming Kingdom.

3. ESCHATOLOGY

(a) The future hope

We come now to the third area of divine disclosure, that of eschatology. For the apocalyptic visionaries there were three great 'saving acts' enacted by God and made known through divine revelation: his creation of the world, his control of history and the coming of his Kingdom. And these three were essentially one. If the God of creation is the God of history, the God of history is the God of 'the last things' who will bring everything to its appointed end. 'In this fashion,' writes André Lacocque concerning the Book of Daniel, 'history is both polarized by a final and historical coming, and suspended in the eternity of divine knowledge and wisdom. This is why the Kingdom of God transcends history and is inserted into history in the reign of the saints (Dan. 7) . . . There is a concordance between heaven and earth . . . Therefore there is a "temporal" concomitance in defeat and ultimate victory that corresponds to the "spatial" concordance of heaven and earth.'[4]

All the signs are that the time is speedily coming when God's sovereign will will be recognized in an act of re-creation and redemption when evil will be utterly destroyed and all wrongs done to his people will be righted. What the Creator has willed and planned at the time of creation will reach its goal in the last days; what he has purposed for his people throughout their long history will find its glorious fulfilment; he will bring to perfection what he has made and rectify what has gone wrong. The End will be as the Beginning and Paradise will be restored. 'In the mystery to come', writes the author of the

Qumran Book of Mysteries, ' . . . wickedness shall retire before righteousness as darkness retires before the light and as smoke vanishes and is no more; so shall wickedness vanish for ever and righteousness appear like the sun.' 'Splendid in every secret thing is thy power', says Enoch, 'from generation to generation, and thy glory for ever and ever; deep are all thy secrets and innumerable, and thy righteousness is beyond reckoning' (I En. 63.3).

Such a hope had of course already found expression in certain Old Testament passages (cf. Isa. 11.6–8; Ezek. 34.25–27) and was an accepted tenet of much oriental and rabbinic literature. In the apocalyptic books, however, it is taken further and elaborated. 'The whole world was created through me,' says the writer of IV Ezra speaking in God's name, 'and through me alone; in the same way, through me and through me alone, the end will come' (6.6); 'then the world will return to its original silence for seven days as at the beginning of creation' (7.30).

The way was being prepared for a remarkable development in the expression of Israel's future hope. This is encapsulated in the phrase 'in the latter end of the days' which referred in the prophets to a time in the distant future when Israel's enemies would be defeated, but in the apocalyptists referred to the immediate future and the termination of history itself. The present world-order would come to an end and be superseded by another of an essentially different kind, presenting a dualistic view of the world in which 'this age' is set over against 'the age to come' (see pp. 107ff) – two expressions with cosmic overtones which they could never have had within the context of Old Testament prophecy. The evil powers with which the world is confronted are no longer simply the great empires and kings of which the prophets had spoken; they are 'principalities and powers in heavenly places'. In such a way apocalyptic eschatology becomes more and more transcendent, laying increasing stress on the supernatural and the supra-mundane. Deliverance comes, not from men, but from God who will bring in his Kingdom and usher in the age to come.

(b) The 'messianic woes'

But before these things come to pass there will be a time of unprecedented woes when the powers of evil will make their last desperate attempt to overthrow the powers of good. The name sometimes given in later Jewish and Christian writings to this period of distress before God's final triumph is 'travail pains of the Messiah'. The picture is familiar to us from our reading of the so-called 'little apocalypse' of Mark 13 (cf. Rev. 12.1–6) where the listed woes are described as 'the beginnings of the birth-pangs' (13.8) – a figure used also in the Dead Sea Scrolls (cf. Hymns III.3–10) and elsewhere to describe the birth of the Kingdom. Even the physical universe itself will be affected; the very stars in heaven will change their courses; the earth will be stricken by earthquake, famine and fire; there will be mysterious portents on the earth and in the heavens reminding men that the End is near.

Sometimes the reference is quite general as in Daniel 12.1: 'And there shall be a time of trouble such as never has been since there was a nation till that time.' At other times it is more detailed and dramatic as in Jubilees 23.13ff.: 'Plague (will come) upon plague, and wound upon wound, and affliction upon affliction, and evil report upon evil report, and sickness upon sickness, and every evil judgment of this sort one with another: sickness and downfall and sleet and hail and frost, and fever and chills and stupor, and famine and death and sword and captivity, and all plagues and suffering' (cf. also I En. 80.2–8; IV Ezra 5.1–13; 6.8–28; 13.30–31; II Bar. 27; 70). All such references show once more that the whole universe, both heavenly and earthly, is a unity; that the cosmos and the course of history are of one piece; and that all things, of whatever kind, will be involved in the coming Great Day when God will bring them to completion.

(c) Participation in the Kingdom

In these books, quite apart from the many preceding 'signs', there is a bewildering variety of eschatological expectation. The Rule of God is sometimes presented as a permanent kingdom here on this earth, purified and restored or else entirely recreated; at other times it appears as a temporary Kingdom on earth, to be replaced by 'the age to come'; and at other times again it seems to be an entirely transcendent realm where men and angels share together in eternal bliss. Sometimes, as we shall see presently, the outlook is nationalistic – God redeems his righteous people and judgment falls on idolatrous nations; at other times it is universalistic and individualistic – men, of whatever race, receive their due reward. There emerges an eschatology which, in the words of Mowinckel, is 'dualistic, cosmic, universalistic, transcendental and individualistic'.[5]

In the main the eschatological hope is expressed in terms of the survival and salvation of the nation of Israel. It is as if the nationalistic hopes that found expression from the time of the Maccabees right down to the fall of Jerusalem in AD 70 were now being projected into the ideal future. The nation of Israel was to fall heir to the Kingdom of God. It is true that in a number of these books a distinction is made on ethical rather than on ethnic grounds (see further pp. 102f., 111ff.): it is 'the righteous' who will inherit the Kingdom. But even here the tendency is to identify 'the righteous' with Israel and 'the wicked' with the Gentiles. In the coming Kingdom the Gentiles will be made to witness the triumph and vindication of God's own people. 'The Kingdom and the dominion,' says Daniel, ' . . . will be given to the people of the saints of the Most High' (7.27).

There is less agreement, however, over the fate of the Gentiles. The hope had been expressed in Old Testament prophecy that the day would come when the nations would look to God and be saved (Isa. 45.20). The holy Temple would be called God's 'house of prayer for all nations' (Isa. 56.7) and his blessing would be shared not only with 'Israel my inheritance', but also with 'Egypt my people' and 'Assyria the work of my hands' (Isa. 19.25). But in other prophecies the Gentiles continued to be presented as the traditional enemies of Israel (Isa. 63.1–6) who would be destroyed by his fury (Isa. 34.1ff.).

It is not surprising that such diverse judgments should find expression in the apocalyptic books also, ranging from a liberal universalism, where the nations share with Israel the blessings of the Kingdom, to their complete destruction and consignment to hell-fire. A generous view is taken in I Enoch where it is said that the Gentiles will be converted by Israel; they will become righteous and offer to God their adoration (10.31), and again in the Testaments of the XII Patriarchs where the archangel Michael intercedes for 'the righteous' who will be spared and given a place in the future age of blessedness (Test. of Levi 5.7; Test. of Napht. 8.3).

Elsewhere, a harder line is followed as in Daniel, other parts of the Testaments of the XII Patriarchs, the Psalms of Solomon and II

Baruch where, although the Gentiles have a place in the future Kingdom, it is in complete subservience to Israel. In other books again, a much harsher view is expressed. There the Gentiles are condemned simply on the ground that they are Gentiles. In the Book of Jubilees, for example, the writer expresses his bitter hatred of them (24.28ff.), and in the Assumption of Moses they are consigned to the flames of Gehenna (10.10). This bitterness finds fullest expression in the Parables of Enoch (37–71) and in IV Ezra. In the Parables, the Gentiles will perish for ever; worms will be their bed; they will be filled with anguish when they look upon the son of man; they will make supplication for mercy, but their prayers will be of no avail, and the righteous will rejoice to see their plight. And in IV Ezra, on the Day of Judgment the Gentile nations will be raised from the dead to be condemned to eternal torment. Such bitterness is no doubt to be understood against the background of much suffering and persecution which the nation of Israel had to endure and, in the case of the later books, no doubt reflects the troubled years that followed the fall of Jerusalem in AD 70.

(d) The transcendence of death

This heading is borrowed from the title of an article by John J. Collins on apocalyptic eschatology in which he makes the following statement: 'In classical biblical prophecy the issue had always been the life of the nation. Apocalyptic still deals with a communal context, whether it be the nation or, more often, the just. However, its concern has extended to the life of the individual. By its focus on heavenly, supernatural realities it provides a possibility that the human life can transcend death, not merely by the future generations of the nation, but by passing to the higher, heavenly sphere. It is this hope for the transcendence of death which is the distinctive character of apocalyptic over against prophecy.'[6] He suggests, then, that apocalyptic eschatology is to be distinguished from prophetic eschatology in at least two important respects.

One is that whereas in prophecy the future hope found expression in communal deliverance or salvation (of the nation or a remnant within the nation), in apocalyptic a new element is introduced alongside the communal, namely, the final salvation of the individual. Some indications of such a hope had already appeared in earlier days, but now it is made quite explicit: the promises of God relating to the time of the end are not restricted to the nation; they are to be realized in the experience of the individual as well.

The break-through came with the writing of the Book of Daniel near the beginning of the second century BC. The historical origin of this is no doubt to be found in the martyrdom of many righteous people in Israel in the time of Antiochus Epiphanes. Such people must surely in some way share in the ultimate triumph of God's people when the time came for him to establish his Kingdom here on earth. There was felt to be a lacuna unless God brought back, raised up, those who had shown themselves to be worthy to take part in his kingly rule. For this to happen, the earth must give birth to them again.

Two Old Testament passages are of particular significance in this connection: Isaiah 24–27 and Daniel 12. In Isaiah 24–27 (a late addition to the Book of Isaiah dating perhaps from the third or fourth century BC) we read: 'Thy dead shall arise; the inhabitants of the dust shall awake and shout for joy, for a dew of lights is thy dew, and the earth shall bring to life the shades' (26.19). If in fact this does refer to an actual resurrection of men's bodies and not to a renewal of the nation, then this is the first occurrence of such a belief in the Old Testament and indicates that the pre-eminently righteous are raised to participate in the Messianic Kingdom to be established on the earth. In Daniel 12, however, we are on more sure historical ground. There we read: 'And many of them that sleep in the dust of the earth shall awake, some to everlasting life and some to everlasting contempt' (12.2). God would raise up these martyrs so that, together with the living, they might share in the blessings of his Kingdom (cf. also II Macc. 7.9, 14, 23, 29). Others among Israel's enemies who had died without receiving due recompense for their wickedness would also be raised to receive the punishment that was their due.

The second distinguishing mark has also been anticipated in the preceding pages. It is that in apocalyptic eschatology there is a change of focus, as it were, from the earthly to the heavenly, a change which first emerges clearly once more in the Book of Daniel. The apocalyptists, in common with many others in their day, shared the mythological notion which saw earthly events in terms of their heavenly counterparts: the struggle between good and evil here on earth was to be understood in terms of the struggle in the heavenly realm between the cosmic forces of light and darkness, between angels and demons, between God and Beliar (see chapter 6). If, as they believed, the truly significant action and the true reality were to be found on the cosmic plain and among the heavenly beings, then 'the chief hope of human beings (must be) to be elevated to this higher sphere of life'.[7] In some apocalyptic writings, says Collins, this transition takes place after death into heaven, often by way of resurrection; in others it takes place before death into a realm where the entrammelling conditions of human life no longer prevail. In either case it can be said that the finality of death has been transcended.

This radical 'change of focus' occurs in the Book of Daniel which now takes a bold and revolutionary step beyond the mythological concept of a mutually interdependent heaven and earth and asserts that the righteous can actually participate in the life of that heavenly sphere and join the company of the angelic host. This will be their ultimate reward – to take their place among the angels, symbolized by the stars of heaven, and to be made into their likeness: 'And the wise shall shine brightly like the splendour of the firmament and those who lead the many to righteousness shall be like the stars for ever' (12.3). They will at last be vindicated and their enemies punished by the justice of God. In such a belief present fear is counteracted by future hope and they are confirmed in their faith. In the long ages past, prophetic visionaries had had only fleeting glimpses of this heavenly realm and of the hidden hosts of God who protected his people Israel. Alone of all the saints of God, only Enoch and Elijah had had permanent access to that realm above. But now it is seen to be the inheritance of all the saints who have remained faithful even to death.

But, argues Collins, this 'transcendence of death' is not only a future hope, it is also a present experience. This is borne out particularly in the texts of the Qumran community.[8] These men presumably believed in some form of life beyond death, although it is difficult to be sure what precise form such survival assumed. What does seem clear is that they believed they had already transcended death, for already they had been 'lifted up to the eternal height'; already they had become part of 'the eternal assembly' and were 'stationed with the host of the holy ones' (1QH III.19–23). Dupont-Sommer and van der Ploeg see in these words an expression of belief in the immortality of the soul. Collins, on the other hand, sees in them an expression of belief in the possession of eternal life here and now. Already here on earth, they enjoyed the life of heaven through their communion with the angel host. Even if this interpretation is correct, however, it does not preclude belief in a future hope and entry into heaven itself. The transcendence of death is assured both here and hereafter.

(e) The nature of survival

It was inevitable that, once the barrier between life and death had been broken down and the future hope was seen in terms of elevation to the heavenly heights, speculation should take over concerning the nature of survival and the form it would assume. This becomes particularly clear when we compare the earlier texts of Daniel, I Enoch and the Qumran writings with, say, IV Ezra, II Baruch and II Enoch. In earlier and later books alike, however, the 'secrets' of the life beyond are made known to the apocalyptic visionary, not least in the heavenly journeys he is privileged to make in which the lot of the departed is clearly revealed.

One noticeable development that takes place is that the departed are no longer simply 'shades' in Sheol, as in the Old Testament; they are 'souls' or 'spirits', separated from one another into different compartments, carefully graded to match their moral and spiritual standing. In the Book of Daniel the distinction between the righteous and the wicked is to be made clear at the time of the resurrection; but in a number of later apocalyptic books it appears beforehand, immediately after death, in Sheol itself. The writer of the Testament of Abraham, for example, tells us that, though all alike are gathered in by the sickle of death (8.10A), a separation is forthwith made between the just and the sinners whose souls are driven through different gates: 'The narrow gate is that of the just, which leads into life . . . The broad gate is that of sinners, which leads to destruction and everlasting punishment' (11.10f.A, cf. Matt. 7.13).

The earliest recorded division into compartments is made in I Enoch

22 (cf. also II Enoch 8–10; Similitudes of Enoch 39.4–8) and finds formalized expression in the Apocalypse of Zephaniah. Reference is made to four such compartments wherein 'the souls of the dead may assemble . . . till the great judgment comes upon them' (22.3). The first is for the spirits of the righteous; the second for sinners who have not in their lifetime received due recompense for the evil they have done; the third is for the righteous who have been martyred; and the fourth is for sinners who have already received punishment in this life for their sins.

Here we have the first reference in this literature to Hell, although the word itself does not occur. Those in the second compartment will be punished in Sheol and then be raised to receive further awful punishment in 'the accursed valley' (27.1), presumably a reference to the Valley of Hinnom – *Ge Hinnom* in Hebrew – from which comes the name Gehenna. Sometimes throughout this literature it refers to Sheol as such; at other times to a compartment within Sheol; and sometimes, as here, to a place of endless torment that follows the final judgment. Over against Gehenna is the Paradise of delight (IV Ezra 7.36; cf. II Enoch 8.1–6; 42.3f.), a veritable Garden of Eden where 'there is no toil, neither grief nor mourning; but peace and exultation and life everlasting' (Test. of Abr. 20.14A).

Most of these books seem to assume that no moral or spiritual response is possible after death. A person's destiny is determined by the life lived here on earth: 'Each of them has prepared for his own soul torment to come, and each of them has chosen for himself glories to come' (II Bar. 54.15). Once inside the gates of Sheol no progress is possible either upwards or downwards. There is no repentance for the souls of the departed (II En. 62.2), nor can the souls of the righteous pray for the living (53.1). As the writer of II Baruch again says, 'There shall not be there . . . a change of ways, nor place for prayer, or sending of petitions, nor receiving of knowledge, nor giving of love, nor place of repentance, nor supplication for offences, nor intercession of the fathers, nor prayer of the prophets, nor help of the righteous' (85.12). In a few books, however, a contrary opinion is expressed; change is envisaged, chiefly through the power of intercessory prayer. Thus the angels pray for the departed Adam (Apoc. of Moses 35.2), and the sun and moon intercede on his behalf (36.1). Great store is set by the prayers of great and godly men like Enoch, Abraham and Moses who, though themselves among the departed, are able to intercede on behalf of others.

In most cases Sheol is regarded as an intermediate state, a place of preliminary rewards and punishments, where the souls of the departed await the resurrection and the final judgment. The wicked are bidden to 'recline in anguish and rest in torment till thy last time come in which thou shalt come again and be tormented still more' (II Bar. 36.11); the righteous, on the other hand, remain unperturbed (even by the torment of the ungodly!); they remain in bliss, guarded by angels till the time of resurrection (IV Ezra 7.95). Elsewhere, however, Sheol itself is seen as the place of judgment as in Jubilees where the spirits of the righteous, immediately after death go to a blessed immortality (22.31) and the spirits of the wicked descend to Sheol, the place of condemnation and darkness (7.29; cf. also I En. 102.5 and 103.78). More often than not, however, the souls of righteous and wicked alike await the day of resurrection and with it the day of judgment.

(f) Resurrection

We have already seen that in the Book of Daniel belief in the transcendence of death expressed itself, not in the form of 'the immortal soul', but rather in the form of 'the resurrected body'. The martyred dead would be raised to inherit the Kingdom, and the wicked would receive their just reward! In the apocalyptic books subsequent to Daniel there is a bewildering variety of belief, not only about the form the resurrection takes, but also about those who will take part in it. Four broad trends may be detected:

First, the righteous alone (or the pre-eminently righteous) are raised to receive their reward, whilst the wicked are consigned to Sheol and final perdition. Thus, in II Enoch the righteous are raised in their 'heavenly' or 'spiritual' bodies in keeping with their spiritual state in Paradise (8.5). Similarly in the Similitudes of Enoch the righteous will 'rise from the earth and cease to be of downcast countenance' (62.15), whereas it is said of the wicked, 'Darkness shall be their dwelling, and worms shall be their bed, and they shall have no hope of rising from their beds' (46.6).

Second, the righteous and the wicked are both raised (as in Daniel) to receive the rewards and punishments they have not received here on earth. This is the scenario in I Enoch 26–27, for example, and in II Baruch where it is said that 'all who have fallen asleep in hope of him shall rise again' (30.1; cf. 51.3) and the bodies of both wicked and righteous shall be transformed, the one to shame and the other to glory (51.3).

Third, the resurrection is universal, to be followed by the judgment. The souls of men will leave their chambers in Sheol and revive their bodies which are restored to life (IV Ezra 7.32).

Fourth, in a few books no reference at all is made to any resurrection. A case in point is Jubilees 23.31: 'And their bones will rest in the earth, and their spirits will have much joy.'

The question remains, however: What kind of body? Several answers are given. Generally speaking, it is believed to correspond to the nature of the Kingdom into which the dead are raised – a physical body for an earthly Kingdom and a spiritual body for a heavenly Kingdom. But such matters obviously puzzled many – as we read in II Baruch: 'Will they then resume this form of the present, and put on these entrammelling members . . . or wilt thou perchance change these things which have been in the world as the world itself?' (49.3). The reply comes back that there will be no change but they will be restored just as they are, with the old physical marks still upon them (50.1–4). A certain ambivalence, however, is to be detected even in this same book which states that, when the judgment is past, the bodies of men will be transformed in a series of changes into spiritual bodies corresponding to their heavenly environment. In II Enoch, the transformation is such that the spiritual body of Enoch needs no food for its satisfaction (56.2); and yet they are related in some fashion to each other, for when he returns to earth for a space of thirty days (presumably in his heavenly body), his face is 'frozen' so that men can recognize him, and he allows the whole assembly to kiss him (64.2–3). This transformed body – like that of the angels in heaven – is often described under the figure of 'garments' or 'garments of light' as in II Enoch 22.8 where Michael is bidden to 'go and take Enoch out of his earthly garments . . . and put him into the garments of my glory' (22.9).

Elsewhere, as in the Apoc. of Moses, the spiritual body in the heavenly Paradise is reckoned to be the counterpart of the physical body in the earthly Paradise (40.2). Not only so, it is co-existent with it as in II Enoch 22.9f. where Enoch's spiritual body, fashioned as a result of his righteous deeds on earth, is to replace his physical body, for, as II Enoch puts it: 'Man is created from invisible and from visible nature; of both are his death and life' (30.10).

(g) The Final Judgment

This belief in the resurrection, whatever form it may take, is closely related to the fact of the coming judgment. This is the great event towards which the whole universe has been moving. As IV Ezra 7.70 puts it: 'When the Most High made the world . . . he first prepared the judgment, and the things that pertain to the judgment.' On that great Day all wrongs will be righted and God's righteous purpose will be vindicated once and for all. Reference to it is made in all the 'historical' apocalypses where, for the most part, it is a judgment of whole peoples rather than of individuals over which God himself presides as Judge (cf. Dan. 7.9–14; I En. 90.20–38).

But alongside this, in Daniel for example, a resurrection of individuals for judgment is also envisaged, a feature particularly prominent in a number of the later apocalyptic writings. According to II Enoch, for example, 'on the day of the great judgment every weight, every measure and every makeweight will be as in the market . . . and according to his measure everyone shall take his reward' (44.5). In the Testament of Abraham (12–14A), where Abel sits on the throne of judgment, the souls of men undergo two tests, one by fire and one by judgment of the balance in which each man's good deeds are weighed against the bad. The destiny of an intermediate class of souls whose merits and sins equally balance depends largely on the prayers of the righteous on their behalf. According to IV Ezra, however, where the judgment scene is graphically depicted (cf. 7.33–38), intercessions for the dead will be of no avail, for 'the day of judgment will be decisive' (7.104) – not only for men and nations, but for angels as well who will be led off to the Abyss of fire (cf. I En. 10.13).

Sometimes the judgment envisaged is catastrophic in character, falling on whole nations and peoples; destruction will come upon the world by water and by fire (Life of Adam and Eve 49.3); the Gentiles will be slain in war and by convulsions of nature (II Bar. 40.1–3). Elsewhere the picture is that of a great Assize, when God will take his seat on the throne and pronounce judgment on the nations of the earth.

In some books two judgments are envisaged, the one preliminary to the other. The first is usually catastrophic and the second forensic. Thus in IV Ezra there will be a judgment of Israel's enemies, to be followed by the great Judgment at the close of the Messianic Kingdom when 'the fires of Gehenna' and 'the Paradise of delight' will be revealed (7.36).

At the heart of all this speculation lies the conviction that God will not allow his people to perish; evil will be punished and good rewarded. The final judgment is the act of one whose eternal purpose will at last be fulfilled.

The reader will have observed that, in the foregoing pages, more space has been given to the subject of eschatology in the apocalyptic writings than to either cosmology or history. Too much, however, should not be read into this for, as Christopher Rowland points out, 'eschatological teaching is certainly to be found in most apocalypses, but it does not demand the close attention from the writer which we are often led to believe'.[9]

Two other matters, which we have looked at only in passing, deserve fuller examination and this will be done in the next two chapters. One is the phenomenon of dualism which has been referred to already in terms of eschatological expectation, but which has much wider ramifications than this. The other is the concept of 'Messiah' and its relation to the expression 'son of man' which, though it is of minor significance within Jewish apocalyptic, occupies a prominent place in Christian eschatology.

VI

Dualism and Apocalyptic

Much of what has been written in the preceding chapters has pointed to a form of dualism in the apocalyptic writings[1] in which a whole series of contrasts appear: God and man, earth and heaven, history and 'beyond history', 'this age' and 'the age to come', wickedness and righteousness, darkness and light, angels and demons, good and evil, God and Satan. Dualism, it can be claimed, is a distinctive mark of Jewish apocalyptic. Nevertheless, we have to be careful in our use of this word within this context. Standing as it does within a distinctly Hebrew tradition, Jewish apocalyptic is essentially monistic in character, never losing the conviction that God the Creator is Lord over the whole creation, be it people or demons or inanimate nature. What we have here is a form of dualism which persistently asserts the sovereignty of Almighty God.

It is true, as we shall see more clearly later, that in grappling with the problem of evil in the world it adopts a theodicy that embraces belief in cosmic demonic powers which usurp the power and authority of God; but such a belief at no time gives cause to deny the fundamental belief in the one God who made heaven and earth and who will one day bring about a new creation. Indeed, these writers go out of their way to make this perfectly plain by declaring that in the beginning it was God the Creator who made 'all the spirits to serve him' (Jub. 2.2); and at the end it is that same God who will be their Judge. From start to finish they are his underlings, entirely subject to his will, unable to do a thing without his permission. Dualism it may be, but it is a dualism that safeguards against all encroachments on the sovereign power of the one, true and only God.

I. WORLDS APART

(a) Two worlds

The apocalyptic writers were conscious of being surrounded by 'another world' of cosmic proportions beyond this present world, far removed from the world of time and sense, where God dwelt with his holy angels. To them he was 'the Most High God', 'the Ancient of Days', 'the Lord of Spirits', 'the Transcendent One', 'the Great Glory' who dwelt in the realm of light, the God of the unutterable name, the God who controlled the destinies of men and nations, the majestic God who would in the end judge all living creatures and bring all things to their completion. He was the high and mighty one who lived in glorious splendour, far removed from the earth in a realm altogether different from our own.

But, as we saw in the previous chapter, there were two 'bridges' whose worth they had proved in their own experience by means of which they were able to come, not only into the presence of God, but also into a knowledge of his divine secrets which he had kept hidden in heaven itself – the dream-visions with their otherworldly journeys and the mediation of angels.

It was a source of great wonder to them that they should have become recipients of such revelations for, as the writer of IV Ezra says, 'Those who dwell upon earth can understand only what is on earth, and he who is above the heavens can understand what is above the height of the heavens' (4.21). They were 'dwellers on earth' who had been given the high privilege of seeing those things 'above the heavens'. Through their God-inspired dreams, visions and translations they were able actually to enter that blessed abode of spirits and commune with angels who interpreted for them the divine mysteries.

The mediation of angels is a very significant feature of these writings, underlining the great gulf that separated earth from heaven and men from God. It is true that they have a role to play within the Old Testament itself; but in the apocalyptic writings of the post-Old

Testament period that role is enormously enhanced, reflecting no doubt the influence of Persian belief and illustrating still further the development of dualistic thought within Judaism as a whole.

Angels are presented as powerful intermediaries between God and men: they disclose divine secrets, they interpret visions and dreams, they carry men's prayers to the throne of God, they encourage and console, they correct and admonish, they execute divine sentence on the great Day of Judgment, they control the elements of nature, they are set over the nations of the earth and rule them as appointed emissaries of the Almighty himself. At the head of this great angelic host stand the archangels, commanders-in-chief as it were of a mighty army whose purpose it is to do the will of the sovereign Lord and to bridge an otherwise unbridgeable gap. The two worlds of earth and heaven were indeed realms apart, but by means such as these they were joined in one.

(b) Two dimensions

This same conviction can be expressed, not only in terms of the two 'worlds' of earth and heaven, but also in terms of the two 'dimensions' of time and space. It will be recalled that, in his definition of 'apocalypse' (see p. 12), J.J. Collins described it as a form of revelatory literature that discloses 'a transcendent reality' to be understood in two dimensions: it is *temporal* (envisaging 'eschatological salvation') and it is *spatial* (involving 'another supernatural world'). The one relates in *horizontal* terms to the events of history and 'the end of history' while the other relates in *vertical* terms to the transcendent, the spiritual, the eternal. They are different from each other, but they are not mutually exclusive. Together they form the framework of apocalyptic vision and apocalyptic speculation.

For the sake of analysis it may be useful to examine them separately. But for the apocalyptic visionaries, in terms of revelation, they belonged together. The two 'horizontal' and 'vertical' dimensions of time and space intersected in such a way that, at the point of intersection, the 'historical' coincided with the 'transcendent', and the 'transcendent' impinged directly and decisively on the 'historical'. This finds illustration in a number of ways. Thus, in the Book of Daniel the transcendent heavenly Kingdom, in the form of a great stone cut out from a mountain 'by no human hand' shatters 'all these (historical, existing) kingdoms and makes an end of them' (Dan. 2.44), i.e. the transcendent values are not confined to some far-distant heavenly realm but have a vital bearing on the hard realities of life – on its politics, its tyrannies, its oppression, its persecution. This is illustrated further in chapter 10 where the 'princes', or guardian angels, of Persia and Greece confront Gabriel, Israel's angelic intercessor, henchmate of Michael 'the prince': these angelic 'princes' are the heavenly counterparts of the peoples and nations over whom they rule; the battles fought by them 'above' reflect and are determinative of the battles fought by men and nations 'below'. This same interplay can be seen even more clearly in the fact that quite frequently angels from the 'vertical' dimension appear as men in the 'horizontal' dimension; and, vice versa, mortal men assume the form of heavenly angels.

The transcendent and the historical, then, have a common identity. The gulf between time and space, like that between earth and heaven, which no mortal man can span, is bridged by God's gift of divine disclosure whereby men can see for themselves the secrets of all the ages.

(c) Two ages
Closely related to these concepts of 'two worlds' and 'two dimensions' is the eschatological dualism of 'two ages', 'this present age' and 'the age to come' – a new order of being, a Golden Age in which all wrongs will be righted and all evil will be destroyed. The difference between them is that, whereas 'the two worlds' which express themselves in 'two dimensions' are seen to be contemporaneous and mutually dependent (cf. Daniel, I Enoch, the Qumran Scrolls), 'the two ages' are seen to be in temporal succession (cf. IV Ezra).

The writer of IV Ezra puts the matter clearly and succinctly in these words: 'The Most High has made not one age but two' (7.50). They are quite different from each other: 'This present age is not the end . . . The Day of Judgment will be the end of this age and the beginning of the immortal age to come, in which corruption has passed away, sinful indulgence has come to an end, unbelief has been cut off, and righteousness has increased and truth has appeared' (7.112ff.).

Only God knows when that new age will dawn; but the apocalyptic writers claim that he has revealed this divine mystery to them and that its coming will be very soon. By far the greatest part of world history, says the writer of IV Ezra, has already passed; only a short time remains (4.4ff.), for '(this) age is hastening swiftly to its end' (4.26). No doubt with the fall of Jerusalem in AD 70 very much in mind, he asserts that the trials of God's people will soon be over. The Golden Age is about to dawn: 'creation is already ageing and passing the strength of youth' (5.55). 'Then (all) time will perish, and afterward there will be neither years nor months nor days nor hours. They will be dissipated, and after that they will not be reckoned. But they will constitute a single age. And all the righteous who escape from the Lord's great judgment will be collected together into the great age. And the great age will come about for the righteous, and it will be eternal. And after that there will be among them neither weariness (nor sickness) nor affliction nor worry nor want nor debilitation nor night nor darkness. But they will have a great light . . . great and incorruptible. For everything corruptible will pass away, and the incorruptible will come into being, and will be the shelter of the eternal residences' (II En. 65.7–10).

But different though they may be, there is a close connection between them, as in the other two concepts we have examined, so that they too tend to merge into each other. Thus, whereas in some apocalyptic writings the coming of the future age will be cataclysmic and catastrophic, accompanied by many signs and wonders, in others the replacement of the one age by the other is a gradual process in which heaven and earth undergo a gradual renewal as men themselves grow in spiritual perception (cf. Jubilees). And whereas in some its coming is seen in terms of the victory of supernatural powers of light over demonic powers of darkness, in others it is seen in terms of a historical process, envisaging the defeat of tyrant-kings and world-empires (cf. Daniel). Referring to the Book of Daniel, André Lacocque comments: 'The scene takes place at least as much on earth and within history as in the heavens and in metahistory . . . The golden age to come begins by being the final stage of human history on this earth. It manifests the triumph of God *in* the triumph of Israel (see I Enoch 102.4–11; 103–104; Wis. 2.1–5; 3.24).'[2]

The two ages, then, are distinct; and yet they are bound together by the common purpose of God which embraces earth and heaven, which reaches through history into eternity and which finds vindication of the 'here and now' in the 'there and then', a vindication which includes not only the righteous nation but the righteous individual as well. In that coming age the temporal world will be taken up into the eternal; 'the present age' will be replaced by 'the age to come'; the course of history will be seen as a crucial part of the eternal divine plan for the cosmos; and God himself will be vindicated once and for all.

2. COSMIC DUALISM

(a) The 'fall' of the angels

In a number of these books the view is clearly expressed that the root cause of evil in 'this present age' is to be found in angelic and demonic powers who have usurped God's rule in the universe. They are given 'free rein', as it were, for a time, but in the end they will be judged by God and be banished or destroyed. Their defeat and subjugation will mark the end of 'this present (evil) age' and the birth of the new age in which God will reign supreme.

Among the apocalypses themselves this 'cosmic dualism' is set forth most fully in I Enoch (cf. chs. 6–19; 64.1f.; 69.4f.; 86.1–6; 106.13–17), Jubilees (cf. 4.15, 22; 5.1–8; 10.4f.) and II Baruch (cf. 56.12–15) and is evident also in other non-apocalyptic books. One popular version, based on the story recounted in Genesis 6.1–6, is contained in I Enoch 6–19. It tells how two hundred angels, called 'Watchers', bound themselves by an oath to take wives from among the children of men and to beget children. They looked down from heaven and 'beheld the daughters of men' and lusted after them (I En. 6.1ff.; Jub. 5.1ff.). To this seduction by the fallen angels was due the depravity of the whole human race and indeed the corruption of the entire universe. The evil progeny which was the fruit of this unholy and unnatural union was 'great giants whose height was 3000 ells' who began to kill one another and to commit all manner of sins against God (I En. 7.2ff.). These giants are called evil spirits as are the creatures which proceed out of their bodies at their death (cf. I En. 15.3, 9f.). It is these fallen angels and their evil brood who are responsible for the tragedies and corruptions of the physical universe – its earthquakes, its pestilences, its diseases, its famines, its storms at sea – and for the perversion and evil in the human heart. It is they, for example, who taught men how to make weapons of war (8.1) with the result that 'the whole earth was filled with blood and oppression' (9.9). Their incitement to sin will continue right up to the Final Day of Judgment.

A variation of the story is given in the Parables of Enoch (I En. 37–71), which tells how, even before the fall of the angels, there was conflict in heaven. There we read of a number of 'Satans', ruled over by a chief Satan, who have access to ' the Lord of spirits' (40.7) and who wage war against him. These rebellious angels, these evil spirits (for such they are), rule over the Watchers who obey their commands and tempt mankind to do all manner of evil on the earth.

Elsewhere, as in II Enoch, the name of the prince of demons is given as Satanail (18.3) who rules over the 'Grigori' and who is described as an archangel who purposed to 'set up his throne higher than the clouds of heaven and be equal in rank with God' (29.4). But God casts him down together with those who support him and he is left 'flying in the air continually above the abyss' (29.5). Some are imprisoned in the second heaven whilst others are cast down to earth where they seduce the daughters of men. On reaching earth their leader Satanail becomes known as Satan where he is determined to create another world and to have lordship over it (31.3). In the Life of Adam and Eve (12–14), he is called the Devil who refuses Michael's order to worship Adam who had been made in the image of God, asserting that Adam ought to worship him because he and not Adam had been made first! In other books he is called by yet other names: as Semjaza he is responsible for all the lawlessness and bloodshed on the earth; as Azazel he 'taught all unrighteousness and revealed the eternal secrets preserved in heaven'; as Mastema he 'leads men astray from the way of God'; and as Beliar or Belial he is 'the prince of deceit'.

(b) *In battle array*

The picture we have, then, is of a great angelic host and an innumerable company of demons under the leadership of a demon prince who has taken control not only of Adam and those who proceed from him, but also of the whole natural universe. Set over against these are myriads of good angels drawn up under the command of the Lord of spirits, ably assisted by seven archangels of whom Raphael and Gabriel, with Michael at their head, are the chief. The relationship of these seven archangels to the seven planets and the description of the angels as stars (which no doubt reflect ancient Babylonian belief) need not concern us here, except to say that they serve to heighten the cosmic nature of this whole scenario.

Satan and his host are in control of this present age. But God's elect and righteous people, in company with his faithful angel band, are assured that the time is coming very soon when there will be a great and final conflict in which they will triumph over the forces of evil. The armies of God will clash with the armies of Satan and judgment will follow. Enoch is given this assurance in a vision which he passes on to 'the elect and the righteous who would be present on the day of tribulation at (the time of) the removal of all the ungodly ones' (I En. 1.1). The time is coming, he tells them, when 'the God of the universe, the Holy Great One, will come forth from his dwelling. And from there he will march upon Mount Sinai and appear in his camp, emerging from heaven with a mighty power. And everyone shall be afraid, and Watchers shall quiver. And great fear and trembling shall seize them unto the ends of the earth' (1.3–5). He will come with ten million of his holy ones to execute judgment (1.9; cf. 16.1; 19.1). The very earth will be rent asunder and there will be a great judgment. The elect will be preserved and the wicked destroyed (1.7ff.). Azazel, a leader among the Watchers, will be 'bound hand and foot and thrown into the darknes' (10.4). In that new age, soon to come, the righteous and elect ones will be vindicated; they will inherit the earth (cf. 5.7) and complete their years in peace (10.17).

3. ETHICAL DUALISM

(a) Two ways

There were other writers, however, for whom the malaise of this present age was to be found, not in the influence of evil cosmic powers, but rather in men's wilful rebellion against God. To them it was essentially an ethical issue in which men and women were faced with a choice between good and evil and in which they were to be held responsible, not only for their own wicked deeds, but also for the wickedness and corruption of the world at large.

The writer of I Enoch 90–105, for example, was aware of the part played by the fallen angels in introducing sin into the world (cf. 100.4); but at the same time he asserted unequivocally that 'sin has not been exported into the world; it is the people who themselves have invented it' (98.4). Other apocalyptic writers like II Baruch and IV Ezra, as we shall see, make no mention of evil angelic powers as the cause of men's sin, emphasizing instead the fact of human responsibility in wrongdoing and the choice human beings are able to make between right and wrong.

According to their judgment, however, such choice was to be made in the light of two important and related factors: the fact of Adam's 'fall' and the involvement in it of all his descendants, and the fact that in every human being there is a propensity to evil in the form of an 'evil inclination' which is basic to human nature itself. Herein lies an ethical form of dualism every bit as marked as that of a cosmological kind.

Adam's sin and ours. The first of these finds clearest reference in II Baruch where, although the writer is aware of the myth of the fallen angels (cf. 56.11–15), he says nothing about any legacy of evil they may have left behind: 'For, although Adam sinned first and has brought death upon all who were not in his time, yet each of them who has been born from him has prepared for himself the coming torment. And further, each of them has chosen for himself the coming glory . . . Adam is therefore not the cause, except only for himself, but each of us has become his own Adam' (54.15, 19). Adam's sin is the cause of both physical (cf. 17.3; 23.4; 54.5) and spiritual (cf. 48.42; cf. IV Ezra 3.21, etc.) death, but this in no way excuses the individual who has still the right of choice between good and ill. The basis of that choice, says the writer, is the Law, obedience to which means life, and rejection of which means death (cf. 54.14). Having the Law, they have no excuse. The choice is theirs. Adam may have been the cause of sin, but they themselves remain responsible for the doing of it.

The evil inclination. The same theme is continued by the writer of IV Ezra who likens the choice men have to make to a contest between two opposing forces within themselves: 'This is the meaning of the contest which every man who is born on earth shall wage, that if he is defeated he shall suffer what you have said, but if he is victorious he shall receive what I have said. For this is the way of which Moses, while he was alive, spoke to the people, saying, Choose for yourself life, that you may live!' (7.127–129), the scriptural reference being to Deuteronomy 30.19 where God says: 'I have set before you life and death, blessing and curse; therefore choose life, that you and your descendants may live.'

This verse of scripture was the motivating influence behind the so-called '*yeçer* theory' which played a significant part in rabbinic theology as well as in a number of the apocalyptic and related writings and the Scrolls from Qumran. It states that in every human being there is an evil *yeçer* or 'inclination' or 'disposition' over against a good *yeçer* in tension with each other, planted in man at birth or at conception by God as a limiting infirmity (cf. Gen. 8.21), but for which man is nevertheless to be held responsible (cf. Gen. 6.5). This is clearly reflected in the Testament of Asher, for example: 'God has granted two ways to the sons of men, two mind-sets, two lines of action, two models and two goals. Accordingly, everything is in pairs, the one over against the other. The two ways are good and evil; concerning them are two dispositions within our breasts that choose between them. If the soul wants to follow the good way, all of its deeds are done in righteousness . . . But if the mind is disposed toward evil, all of its deeds are wicked; driving out the good, it accepts the evil' (1.6, 8). The word *yeçer*, says Benedikt Otzen, reveals 'a sliding scale of meanings, ranging from the more or less neutral "free will" to the negatives "drive" or "lust" . . . The "freewill" or "impulse" is the locus within the human personality where the battle between good and evil takes place. It is also the locus where people sometimes surrender in the face of evil . . . Human beings are both free and, somehow, unfree; they will the good, but are in the clutches of their senses.'[3] (Cf. Rom. 7.15ff.)

This is the theme also of IV Ezra where, however, the 'evil inclination' is described as 'an evil root' in Adam that bears fruit in 'the evil heart', alienating men and women from God (cf. 7.48). A key passage in this connection is 3.21f.: 'For the first Adam, burdened with an evil heart, transgressed and was overcome, as were also all who were descended from him. Thus the disease became permanent . . . What was good departed and the evil remained.' This 'evil heart', which alienates men from God, is transmitted from Adam to his descendants: 'O Adam, what have you done? For, though it was you who have sinned, the fault was not yours alone, but ours also who are your descendants' (7.118). Even though the blame lies at Adam's door, no attempt is made to explain the actual connection between his sin and that of his descendants who remain responsible for their wrongdoing.

Here again, as in II Baruch, reference is made to God's giving of the Law as a remedy for men's ills, for 'the Law was in people's heart along with the evil root' (3.22). The plight they find themselves in is their own fault, for 'they received freedom, but they despised the Most High, and were contemptuous of his Law and forsook his ways' (8.55f.). Obedience to the Law will ensure 'a treasure of works laid up with the most High' (7.77; cf. 8.33). Adam's sin, 'the evil root' and 'the evil heart' may indeed incline men to sin, but in the end the choice remains between the way of life and the way of death. The Law offers the way of salvation and accountability remains.

(b) Two spirits

Elsewhere in these writings (particularly in Jubilees, the Testaments of the XII Patriarchs and the Qumran Scrolls) this same duality is expressed in the form of 'two spirits' at enmity with each other in the world and in the human heart. Thus, in the Testament of Judah it is said, 'Two spirits await an opportunity with humanity: the spirit of truth and the spirit of error' (20.1). Sometimes these correspond to 'the evil inclination' and 'the good inclination' in man; but at other times they are personalized and correspond rather to 'the angel of darkness' who is called Satan or Beliar or some other such name, and 'the angel of light' to be identified with the archangel Michael who leads his people in the light into the paths of truth.

This belief is expressed clearly in the Qumran Scrolls where we read: '(God) has created man to govern the world, and has appointed for him two spirits in which to walk until the time of His visitation: the spirits of truth and falsehood . . . All the children of righteousness are ruled by the Prince of Light and walk in the ways of light; but all the children of falsehood are ruled by the Angel of Darkness' (1QS III.17–19). In the Scrolls, then, as in other related writings, evil is described in terms both of two conflicting dispositions in human nature and of two conflicting cosmic forces at work in this present evil age. Within the same context we have both wilful human transgression and enforced demonic subjection, both forensic trial and cosmological judgment, both individual retribution and corporate election, both salvation through the Law and deliverance by means of angels.

Throughout these writings, then, there is a marked ambivalence between the 'two spirits' that arise from within and those that originate from without. This in turn highlights the dilemma between predetermination by external forces beyond man's control and his free choice of right or wrong. To the apocalyptic writer, however, as indeed to Judaism as a whole, this dilemma was more apparent than real. The cosmic forces were indeed a powerful factor; but, in the ultimate, sin is not given 'from above', but comes from man himself (cf. I En. 98.4; Greek text). Or, as Ben Sira puts it more bluntly: 'When the ungodly man curses Satan, he is (really) cursing himself' (21.27). Satan may be hard at work; but you cannot blame him for the wrong you do. Is there free-will? The apocalyptist, and others like him, might well reply: 'Categorically, yes! You have no choice!!'

VII

Messiah and 'Son of Man'

Throughout the intertestamental period there was much speculation concerning the coming of the Messianic Kingdom which would be inaugurated by God himself, sometimes with and sometimes without the help of his Messiah. Speculation within the apocalyptic writings concerning the nature and identity of the Messiah is very limited if only because relatively little attention is paid there to the Messiah as such. In a few cases, when he does make an appearance, the role he plays is a fairly limited one. Some of the evidence would, at first sight, seem to support the view that he assumes the form of a heavenly, pre-existent being, but closer examination shows that in all probability he is to be seen as a mortal man and no more. We shall look at some of this evidence, sparse though it is, and see if this conclusion is justified. But first we shall consider quite briefly the popular expectation of the time.

1. EXPECTATION AND SPECULATION[1]

(a) As king and priest
The general and popular messianic expectation in Palestine at the beginning of the Christian era was that of a victorious warrior-king, a strong-arm saviour who, by military might, would rid the country of its hated enemies and set the people free from tyranny and oppression. He would destroy godless nations, and the heathen would be made to

serve under his yoke, bringing with them as gifts God's exiled people (cf. Pss. of Sol. 17.23ff.).

It is perhaps not surprising, however, that, during those centuries when the priestly Maccabees and their successors the Hasmoneans assumed kingly rule, the conviction was expressed, in some circles at any rate, that the Messiah would be a priestly figure, sometimes alongside a kingly figure and at other times in his own right, taking upon himself kingly authority (cf. Test. of Levi 18.2–9; Test. of Judah 24.5–6). Such a belief is reflected in the Community Rule from Qumran which refers to 'a prophet and the *Messiahs* of Aaron and Israel' (1QS ix.11), and in the Testimonies Scroll (4Q Testimonia) which quote biblical texts with specific reference to the messianic hope (Deut. 5.28f.; 18.8f.; 33.8–11; Num. 24.15–17). Precedence is given in the Scrolls, as in the Testaments, to the priestly figure over against the kingly, reflecting no doubt the priestly character of the Qumran Community itself.

(b) Two eschatological prophets

It is clear, from a number of sources at this time including the New Testament, that there was a popular expectation that, in the days leading up to the End, a prophet would arise who would herald the coming of the Messianic Kingdom (cf. I Macc. 4.46; 14.41). This expectation found expression in two Old Testament figures, Elijah who would appear 'before the great and terrible day of the Lord comes' (Mal. 4.5), and Moses who had promised that God would raise up a prophet like himself (cf. Deut. 18.15, 18).

According to Ben Sira, Elijah was a great messianic figure who would 'calm the wrath of God' and 'restore the tribes of Jacob' (48.10). He was not himself the promised Messiah but his forerunner, as is seen for example in his identification by some people with John the Baptist (cf. Luke 3.15; John 1.20). The hope was expressed, not so much in the return of Elijah himself, as in the coming of a prophet imbued with the spirit and power of Elijah (cf. Luke 1.17). In course of time, however, the belief arose that Elijah himself would return to earth as a heavenly visitor to herald the Messiah. A passage sometimes quoted in support of this is I Enoch 90.31, where Elijah, together with Enoch, is said to come down from heaven in readiness for the judgment and the coming of the Messiah. James D.G. Dunn, however, judges that what we have here is simply a case of 'a visionary scene-changing' and does not in fact indicate the coming of a heavenly deliverer for which there is no clear evidence before the end of the first century AD.[2] Allusion to the Messiah himself is made a few verses later, in 90.37, under the symbol of a white ox with huge black horns in whose presence the onlookers tremble. The reference is quite incidental and indicates a human figure who apparently has little or no involvement in the inauguration of the Kingdom or the progress of the age to come.

Hope was also expressed in the coming of 'a prophet like Moses' who would herald the coming of the Kingdom. In the Community Rule and in the Testimonies Scroll from Qumran, as we have already noted, he is mentioned alongside 'the Messiahs of Aaron and Israel' and may have been identified, in the minds of the Qumran Community, with their Teacher of Righteousness. There is ample evidence in the Gospels for belief in such a prophet in the first part of the first century AD (cf. John 1.20). There were those who saw the fulfilment of this prophecy in Jesus himself (cf. John 6.14, 7.40; Acts 3.22, 7.37), a designation, however, which seems to have fallen out of favour at a fairly early stage as a result, perhaps, of the antics of certain self-designated prophets in Palestine at that time who not only claimed to be the prophet promised of old but who also claimed to be able to perform miracles like those performed by Moses in the wilderness (cf. Acts 5.36 and *Ant.* XX.97; Acts 21.38 and *Ant.* XX.167f.).

(c) *The Messiah in heaven*

So far we have observed that, in the literature of the period and particularly in the apocalyptic literature, the figure of the Messiah is given a relatively low profile, and we have seen no reason to doubt that he appears there simply as a mortal man. We come now to what appears to be a quite different kind of speculation concerning the Messiah who, it is suggested, is to remain hidden in heaven until the time when he will come to earth to establish his Kingdom. There are three apocalyptic writings of particular interest in this connection: the Similitudes of Enoch (I En. 37–71), II Baruch and IV Ezra. We shall reserve consideration of the first of these for the moment and examine the evidence it provides in connection with the expression 'son of man', and look at the other two, dating from around the end of the first century AD.

Two key passages in this connection are II Baruch 30.1 and IV Ezra 14.9. In the former we read: 'When the time of the Messiah has been fulfilled (presumably in his earthly Kingdom), he will return (presumably to heaven) in glory', where the word 'return', it is argued, indicates that he had been there already in his pre-Kingdom state. In the latter reference it is said that Ezra will be 'taken up from among men . . . and will remain with my son', meaning the Messiah himself. These two passages, it has been argued, taken together or separately, seem to suggest a doctrine of the Messiah's pre-existence in heaven.

Strong counter arguments, however, have been put forward that this is a mistaken judgment and that the Messiah is not the heavenly, transcendent pre-existent figure he appears to be. Behind the descriptions given in these texts, it is claimed, lies the rabbinic tradition that seven things were created before the world was made, one of which was 'the name of the Messiah'. So central were such things in the mind and purpose of God from the very beginning that they were seen by the rabbis as having existed from eternity, from before the creation of the world. G.F. Moore emphasizes that what is mentioned here as preceding the world is not the *person* of the Messiah but the *name* of the Messiah.[3] Geza Vermes makes the same point and comments:

> Some may be tempted to see in this Messiah an eternally pre-existent, heavenly Christ; but no such conclusion is warranted. The surviving sources are concerned only with a notional pre-existence of the Messiah in so far as his 'name', i.e. his essence and nature, preceded the formation of light by God on the first day of Creation.[4]

This conclusion finds confirmation elsewhere in these same two apocalyptic books where it is made clear that the Messiah they have in mind is in fact an earthly, human figure in keeping with the kingly Messiah of common Jewish expectation. This is the picture given in II Baruch, for example, despite a measure of inconsistency in the information given. After the fall of three of the four great empires referred to in Daniel 7, says the writer, 'the principate of the Messiah will be revealed' (39.7). The fourth empire (identified here presumably with Rome) will then be destroyed and its ruler brought before the Messiah for judgment (40.1f.). The principate of the Messiah will then stand for ever. It is an earthly Kingdom which will last as long as the earth itself endures (40.3). Elsewhere in the book (chs 53ff.) the Messiah will come and summon the nations, some of whom he will spare and some he will destroy (72.2). A somewhat different picture is given in chapters 27ff. where the Kingdom is to be established on an idealized earth where 'on one vine there will be a thousand branches, and each branch will produce a thousand clusters, and each cluster will produce a thousand grapes, and each grape will produce a cor of wine' (29.5). This glorious earthly kingdom will come to an end and with it all corruption; a new age of blessedness and incorruption will be ushered in (44.12). And 'when the time of the Messiah is fulfilled, he shall return (to heaven?) in glory. Then all who have fallen asleep in him shall rise again' (30.1).

A somewhat similar picture is given in IV Ezra, although here again there is a lack of consistency. In the so-called Eagle Vision, for example, in 10.60–12.35, the writer gives a reinterpretation of the vision recorded in Daniel 7 in which a lion appears and destroys the eagle symbolizing the Roman empire (11.37; 12.1ff.). The lion represents the great deliverer of the coming age and is called 'the Messiah . . . who shall spring from the seed of David' (12.32), i.e. he is the earthly Davidic Messiah of common expectation. This identification of him as a human Messiah is made even more explicit in 7.28–29 where we read: 'It shall be, after those days, that my servant the Messiah shall die' (7.29), i.e. he is a mortal man.

It will be clear, then, from what has been said, that the apocalyptic writers were not unduly concerned about the character or even the function of the Messiah, nor did they engage in overmuch speculation on this account. To them, if mentioned at all, he was a man like other men, chosen by God to take part in the triumph of the Kingdom.

2. MESSIAH AND 'SON OF MAN'

(a) The expression 'son of man'

We come now to a subject over which much ink has been spilt and about which there is much controversy still among scholars because of its significance for christology and New Testament study. This is not our particular concern here; we shall confine ourselves to the evidence of the Jewish apocalyptic sources. The question at issue is this: What is the connection between this expression and the eschatological or messianic figure that emerges in due course out of reflection on Daniel 7.13, and in particular is it to be taken as a title or simply as a description of the one so described?

In an earlier work I have attempted an analysis of the texts concerned and shall not repeat unnecessarily what was said there.[5] It will become clear, however, that I have altered my earlier position when I accepted the expression as a title given to a transcendent, heavenly being. On further reflection I now accept it as descriptive rather than as titular and so shall refer to it without the use of capital letters simply as 'son of man'. I tend to agree with Geza Vermes, for example, who, after a thorough examination of the relevant sources, states that 'no trace survives (in Aramaic usage) of its titular use, from which it must be inferred that there is no case to be made for an eschatological or messianic office-holder generally known as "the son of man"'.[6] But of course language is not the only factor to be considered; the exegesis of Daniel 7.13 must be taken into account and to that we now turn.

(b) In Daniel 7.13

There can be no doubt that Daniel 7 was a key factor in the development of future speculation concerning the figure described as 'the son of man' or 'one like a son of man'. We note, however, that no mention is made here of the Messiah as the deliverer of his people and that, in particular, the figure of the 'son of man' does not assume this role. In a night-vision, we are told, 'one like a son of man was coming with the clouds of heaven' (7.13) and was brought near to the Ancient of Days who gave him 'sovereignty, glory and kingship' (7.14). A few verses later, in 7.18, it is stated that this triumphant status is to be given to 'the saints of the Most High', an expression generally taken as referring to the people of God who would inherit the coming Kingdom, i.e. on this interpretation the 'son of man' is a symbolic figure and not a real figure, and is to be interpreted in a corporate sense with particular reference to the coming Kingdom and its embodiment in the people of God. The Gentile nations, represented by the four great beasts, will be destroyed by God's people, represented by the figure of 'a man' (for this is what the Aramaic idiom means) who will receive from God's hand a Kingdom which will have no end.

Strong arguments, however, have been brought forward, helpfully set out by Christopher Rowland for example,[7] that the 'one like a son of man' does indeed represent a real figure and is that of an angelic being. Such an identification finds support, not only in the comparison made here with a man – he is 'one like a (son of) man – but also by the fact that, in the apocalyptic writings and elsewhere, the human figure is quite often taken to represent an angel (e.g. Dan. 8.15) just as animals are taken to represent human beings. An additional supporting factor is that the reference to his coming 'with the clouds of heaven' is commonly associated in the Old Testament with the presence of a divine being.

But can this angelic figure be identified still further? There are in fact indications here and elsewhere that he is none other than the archangel Michael himself. Such an identification is made implicitly in chapter 7 and explicitly in several places throughout chapters 8–12.[8] We know from Daniel 12.1 that Michael is the guardian angel of Israel, and in the War Scroll from Qumran we read these significant words: 'He (God) will send eternal succour to the company of his redeemed by the might of the princely Angel of the kingdom of Michael . . . He will raise up the kingdom of Michael in the midst of all flesh'.[9] (See also the reference in Revelation 12.2 to Michael's part in the coming of the Kingdom in his slaying the Dragon.)

If this identification is correct, we are to see in Michael the heavenly representative and counterpart of the earthly people of God mentioned in 7.18 as 'the saints of the Most High'. His vindication in heaven is both a sign and a pledge of their vindication on earth and an assurance that they will triumph in the end when they will receive the Kingdom. On such an understanding, then, there is no hint here of the 'son of man' being identified with the Messiah, transcendent or otherwise, or of any doctrine of a heavenly-saviour who will come to earth to save his people.

(c) Later messianic interpretation

It is perhaps not surprising, however, that subsequent writers were to find in Daniel 7 suitable material from which to build such a belief and to construct such a doctrine. 'There is no evidence,' writes E.W. Heaton, 'that the writer ever thought of a messianic leader . . . but when, later, such an interest did arise it is understandable that there should have been close connection between (and therefore terminology common to) the People of God referred to here, and the individual figure who came to be thought of as its principal and embodiment.'[10] Two apocalyptic books are of particular significance in trying to trace any such development within Jewish thought at that time: IV Ezra and the Parables of Enoch contained in I Enoch 37–71.

We have already seen how, in the Eagle Vision contained in IV Ezra 10.60–12.35 the writer gives a reinterpretation of the 'son of man' in Daniel 7.13 in terms of the historical Davidic Messiah. Another messianic allusion is made in the so-called Vision of the Man from the Sea contained in chapter 13 where he appears in 'the form of a man' (13.3) or as 'the man' (13.5, 15) or 'this man' (13.3). In a dream the seer sees a storm-tossed sea, and coming out of it 'as it were the form of a man' who 'flew with the clouds of heaven' (13.1–3). A great multitude assemble to make war against him, but he destroys them with 'a fiery stream' that comes forth from his mouth (13.10). The ten captive tribes are united with the other two and enjoy the kingdom of peace (13.48). He it is whom 'the Most High is keeping many ages and through whom he will deliver his creation' (13.26). Everything that pertains to him is a divine secret, for 'just as one can neither search nor know what is in the depth of the sea, even so can no one upon earth see my Son, but in the time of his day' (13.52). In him the mysteries of God's purpose are concealed, but when he appears, what is hidden will at last be revealed.

This dream is obviously modelled on Daniel 7.13. In neither case, we observe, is the expression 'son of man' used as a title; but in IV Ezra, unlike Daniel, it is now interpreted with reference to the

Messiah. But what kind of Messiah? The description given in these verses might lead us to imagine that he is presented here as a heavenly, transcendent being who will come from heaven as the saviour of his people. Such an interpretation, however, would sit very uneasily with the picture given in the same book of a Messiah who would in the end die as other men die (cf. 7.29). The solution, it has been suggested, is to be found in the fact that, whereas in Daniel 7 we have a theophany in which a real figure is represented by the 'son of man', in IV Ezra 13 we have a vision in which the 'son of man' has no corresponding reality in heaven but is used simply as a symbol of the Messiah who will, in the days to come, judge the nations and deliver his people.[11]

The second text of importance in this connection is the Parables of Enoch (I En. 37–71). An examination of these chapters is fraught with many difficulties, not least because of their apparently composite character and the determination of their date. J.T. Milik, for example, takes them to be 'the work of a Jew or a Jewish Christian of the first or the second century AD'.[12] (This is the only section of I Enoch of which no trace is found among the Dead Sea Scrolls.) Geza Vermes agrees to a post-AD 70 date as in the case of IV Ezra.[13] There is division of scholarly opinion on this point, however, and others would date them variously between the years 100 BC and AD 70.[14] This question of dating is obviously of considerable importance for the christological debate arising out of Jesus' use of the expression 'son of man'; our present concern, however, is simply to ascertain what form or forms speculation on Daniel 7.13 assumed in the Parables, whatever date may be assigned to them. There are many other problems, besides that of dating, of a philological and exegetical kind that are relevant to the whole debate but which are not our particular concern here.

In the second Parable we are introduced to a heavenly figure bearing the title 'the Elect One' (45.3), and elsewhere 'the Righteous One' (38.2; 53.6), who 'on that day . . . shall sit on the seat of glory' (45.3). A few verses later, in a passage clearly reminiscent of Daniel 7, he is referred to as ' the son of man who has righteousness and with whom righteousness dwells' (46.3). Two observations may be made here. One is that, although the terms 'the Elect One' and 'the Righteous One' are titles, the term 'son of man' is not but is simply a reference back to 'the Elect One' who is 'full of grace, like one of the holy angels'

(46.1). He is one who had been 'given a name before the creation of the sun and the moon, before the creation of the stars' (48.3), i.e. he had been in the mind and purpose of God from the beginning (see p. 119 above).

The second observation is that this 'son of man' who is 'the Elect One' is described in terms that are reminiscent of the Davidic king (cf. 46.5f.; 49.3) and on two occasions is actually designated 'Messiah' (48.10, 52.4). The time will come when this 'son of man' will be seen 'sitting on the throne of his glory. Kings, governors and all landlords shall bless, glorify and extol him who rules over everything'. He who has been concealed from the beginning will at last be revealed to the holy and elect ones who will abide with God and be with him for all eternity (cf. 62.5–14). Here, then, we have the application of the word 'Messiah' to a heavenly figure, 'the Elect One', referred to as 'son of man', who will serve as eschatological judge.

Another intriguing reference that has caused no small controversy is contained in chapter 71 where the 'son of man' is identified with none other than Enoch himself. In his ascent to heaven he is addressed by one of the angels in these words: 'You are the son of man who was born in righteousness and upon whom righteousness dwells' (71.14). Here we have the identification of the 'son of man' with a human being who has been exalted to heaven where he serves as a heavenly judge – a fitting climax, it might be said, to the career of one who is presented in the First Book of Enoch as a celestial scribe whose responsibility it was to record 'the condemnation and judgment of the world' (Jub. 4.23). The claim that this means the adoption of the expression 'son of man' as a messianic *title* is another matter altogether.

Writing of this identification of Enoch with the 'son of man' Geza Vermes draws this conclusion:

> No other inference is logical except to identify the heavenly Enoch with the son of man=the Messiah. More concretely, . . . the name of the Messiah, i.e. the Messiah not yet 'real' but awaiting the predestined moment of his birth, is henceforth incarnate in the heavenly body of Enoch, and sitting next to God, acts as his chief assistant.[15]

A number of scholars, however, would see in this heavenly figure a reference to none other than the archangel Michael with whom Enoch is to be identified here. Just as 'the Righteous One' is counterpart of 'the righteous ones' on earth, so the 'son of man' may be regarded as the counterpart of the supreme representative of 'the righteous' on earth, namely 'the righteous Enoch'. Such an identification of Enoch with an angelic or archangelic figure is not as far-fetched as it might appear to be when we observe that, in two other books that bear his name, II and III Enoch, an account is given of his exaltation to the rank of archangel. In the second of these two books he is actually identified with the archangel Metatron (cf. III Enoch 4.2) who is also called 'the lesser Yahweh' (III Enoch 12.5).

An interesting contribution to this 'son of man' debate is made by the so-called Melchizedek fragment (11Q Melchizedek) found at Qumran. There Melchizedek, the mysterious 'priest of the most high God' (Gen. 14.18; Ps. 110.4) is identified with the archangel Michael in a judgmental and redemptive role. Matthew Black affirms[16] that the Enoch=son of man apocalyptic tradition in the Parables (as well as a Michael=son of man tradition) has a parallel here in a Melchizedek= Michael apocalyptic tradition and leaves it as an open question which of these came first.

Out of this cursory examination we may reach a number of conclusions. One is simply to re-affirm what has already been said that the expression 'son of man' is not used as a title, messianic or otherwise, in these Jewish writings.

Second, though not messianic in its Daniel origins, in course of time it acquired a clear messianic connection in such books as IV Ezra and the Parables of Enoch.

Third, in the Parables the name 'Messiah' is given to a heavenly figure, 'the Elect One', who is referred to as 'son of man'.

Fourth, the identification of Enoch with the 'son of man' in the Parables indicates that, at the time when these chapters were written, whenever that may have been, 'the son of man concept involved the idea of a person exalted in the heavens with a previous historical existence'.[17]

Fifth, all of this has a bearing on Jesus' use of the term. This is not our particular concern in these pages, but two conclusions drawn by J.D.G. Dunn[18] in this connection are worth noting. The first is that the earliest traceable interpretation of Daniel 7.13 in terms of a particular individual goes back to earliest Christianity or to Jesus himself. And the second is that this interpretation probably originally emerged as a way of expressing either Jesus' own hope of vindication or the first Christians' belief that Jesus had been vindicated after death and would soon 'come with the clouds of heaven'.

VIII

Apocalyptic Interpretation: A Christian Perspective

I. IN THE NEW TESTAMENT

(a) An apocalyptic framework

It is not the object of this book to examine or expound Christian, as distinct from Jewish, apocalyptic whose influence was felt from an early date within the Christian church. But some reference, however brief, is called for in view of the continuity which obviously existed between the two. From an early date, it would seem, Jewish apocalyptic writings were interpolated in such a way as to give them a Christian interpretation and specifically Christian apocalypses were written; one of these, the Book of Revelation, found its way into the canon of the New Testament itself. These Christian apocalypses had much in common with the Jewish works, the chief difference being that they focussed on the revelation of God made known through Jesus Christ their Lord.

There is good reason to believe that Jesus was born into, and that the early church grew up in, a religious atmosphere that was influenced by apocalyptic thought. 'While it may be true,' writes Christopher Rowland, 'that some of the characteristic features of the apocalypses are absent from the teaching of Jesus and are replaced by the parables, it would seem to be a mistake to suppose that Jesus remained unaffected by the thought-world of apocalyptic', and adds that 'there is indeed evidence to suggest that on certain occasions (he) received visions which resemble the visions of apocalyptic'.[1]

We think particularly in this connection of Jesus' preaching concerning the Kingdom of God and that quality of transcendence that differentiates it from a purely 'political' concern, the 'signs and wonders' that are to precede the End-time, the 'messianic woes' that are to accompany it, 'the age to come' set over against 'this present age', the struggle between the cosmic powers of light and darkness which strive for control of the world, the defeat of Satan and his evil progeny, and the ultimate triumph of God whose sovereign power is supreme over all his creation.[2]

Or we think of the coming of the Kingdom as a 'mystery' to which reference is made in the Jewish apocalyptic books. In Mark 4.11, for example, Jesus chooses to reveal the secrets of the Kingdom to the inner circle of his disciples in a typically apocalyptic manner: 'To you has been given the secret of the Kingdom of God, but for those outside everything is in parables.' He himself is the key to that mystery just as he is the key to the interpretation of scripture in which the mystery is concealed. According to Paul it was a mystery that 'was kept secret for long ages but is now disclosed' (Rom. 16.25f.) and has now been made known (cf. Rom. 16.25; Eph. 3.3, 8ff.), which is 'Christ in you the hope of glory' (Col. 1.26f.). Not only in the Gospels, then, but in the letters of Paul as well the influence of apocalyptic is to be clearly detected, both in the mode of the revelations received, and in the thought-forms in which he expressed his faith in Christ.[3]

In such ways as these the eschatological teaching of Jesus and its interpretation by Paul is presented in the thought-form of Judaism in general and Jewish apocalyptic in particular. It was against the background of apocalyptic expectation that Jesus came into Galilee declaring, 'The time is fulfilled and the Kingdom of God is at hand,' and it was against this same background that the early church was to interpret his coming and his coming again.

(b) The transformation of apocalyptic
But the really significant thing to note is not so much the influence of apocalyptic on Jesus and the early church as it was the influence of Jesus and the early church on apocalyptic. This is expressed epigrammatically by Gerhard Ebeling in these words: 'We do not merely interpret Jesus in the light of apocalyptic, but also and above all we interpret apocalyptic in the light of Jesus.'[4] The religious form

in which the apocalyptic writers had preserved and passed on their faith, valuable though it was, was not adequate to express the hopes and expectations of Jesus and his followers who, though they adopted much of its language and expression, transformed it completely in the process.

There is evidence, then, of apocalyptic influence in the teaching of the Gospels and the rest of the New Testament. It is significant, however, that actual writings with a marked apocalyptic identity are in fact very few in number. Within the Gospels themselves there are only two sizeable contributions – Mark 13 (with parallels in Matthew 24 and Luke 21.5–36) and Luke 17.20–37. But even these show as many differences as they do similarities when compared with Jewish apocalyptic. In Mark 13.32, for example, Jesus goes out of his way to decry speculation concerning the time of the end and to refute all attempts to predict the hour of its coming.

But of course the outstanding example of the influence of apocalyptic in the New Testament is to be found in the Book of Revelation where the visionary mode of revelation is hardly to be distinguished from that of the Jewish apocalypses. It is significant, however, that it did not make its appearance until around the end of the first century and that, for a time, it met with a mixed reception. Here again the differences as well as the similarities are most marked. The writer does not feel obliged, for example, to write in the name of some illustrious figure of the past. He has not received his revelation from of old, nor has it been recorded and preserved for long ages in secret books. He has no need to conceal his identity behind a pseudonym: he is a prophet called John (cf. 1.1; cf. 22.7) who has received from God a direct revelation of Jesus Christ which he is now communicating to his fellow Christians throughout Asia Minor. This marked difference between Revelation and its Jewish counterparts is to be found, moreover, not just in its form, but also in its content which is concerned from beginning to end with the person and work of Jesus, the crucified, risen and exalted Son of God. There he is portrayed, not in apocalyptic fashion as either Warrior-Messiah or fire-breathing 'man from heaven', but as a lamb that had been slain (cf. Rev. 5.6). It is as the suffering witness that Jesus bears testimony to God's sovereign rule. The cruciform reshaping of popular apocalyptic spoke critically to all who might be tempted to scan the heavens for signs of the Kingdom's coming or to live with false notions of what that coming meant.

Such transformation of apocalyptic finds ample evidence in the Gospels themselves. In his teaching concerning the Kingdom, for example, Jesus makes it plain that to detect the hand of God in history and in everyday life is infinitely more important than to identify portents, signs and wonders and to calculate the time of the End and the coming of that Kingdom. It is to be sought, not in prognostications or as the foreordained climax to history, but in the sovereign rule of God that is breaking into history and into the human heart in the here and now.

Entry into the Kingdom, moreover, is bound up inseparably with the person of Jesus himself and with his eschatological offering of the forgiveness of sins to as many as repent and believe. The 'mystery' or 'secret' of the Kingdom is that it is to be appropriated through faith in him. In him the Kingdom has come and through him it will reach its consummation. To be 'in Christ', as Paul would put it, is to be in the Kingdom.

But the Kingdom is related not only to the person of Jesus, but also – and in a very special way – to his vicarious work of redemption on the cross. The message of the Book of Revelation in this regard surely reflects the mind of Jesus himself who, there is reason to believe, interpreted his messiahship in terms of the Suffering Servant of Isaiah 53. To him the cross was inevitable if the 'mystery' was to become 'an open secret'. Jesus died in order that the Kingdom might come 'with power' (Mark 9.1; cf. Rom. 1.4).

To sum up this brief account we quote some apposite words of E.F. Scott:

Down even to details the conventional features of the apocalyptic hope appear in His (i.e. Christ's) teaching. But while he thus accepted the idea of the kingdom as He found it, He employed it only as a framework for his own original message. The speculative problems on which the thought of Enoch, Baruch and 4th Esdras is mainly centred have little interest to him. He refuses to assign a date to the final consummation or to solve any of the riddles concerning the nature of future life . . . Adopting though he does the current eschatological ideas, he is at no pains to combine them in a consistent picture.[5]

2. CRITERIA OF INTERPRETATION

We turn now from the New Testament to a consideration of the abiding value of the apocalyptic message in our modern world, and in so doing we have come full circle, as it were, to pick up what was said in the Introduction concerning the affinity that exists between the events which were the occasion of these ancient Jewish (and Christian) apocalypses and the events of today. Our study of these texts and the beliefs set forth in them has been, for the most part, an academic exercise. But something more than this is involved: it is at the same time a search for meaning behind the hopes and fears expressed in these books. To uncover such meaning the texts require interpretation, and for this I would suggest three useful criteria:

(a) The integrity of the texts

In trying to interpret the message of apocalyptic we have first of all to recognize the integrity of the literature concerned within its own religious, historical, political and cultural setting. We have to ask what the writer of a particular book was trying to say to the people of his own generation and within the situation in which he found himself. The message of the book was bound up inseparably with the times in which it was first written. God speaks and acts in history and through history to specific situations, and it is within that context and not isolated from it that we are to interpret the message of this book and that.

This is particularly so in the case of a book like that of Daniel where the temptation of many has been to cut it off from its historical moorings, as it were, and to give its message an interpretation altogether detached from its original meaning, with sometimes dire results. A case in point is that of the vastly popular writings of Hal Lindsey[6] in the United States who adopts a fundamentalist and literalist stance and expounds scripture (particularly apocalyptic scripture) with little or no consideration of the social, political, cultural or religious soil from which it sprang, interpreting it in a purely subjective way and applying it to specific, named events or people or nations in our own time. Such an approach refuses to take history seriously or to recognize, as the Bible itself does, that its teaching is embedded in history and cannot be understood aright apart from its historical context. It has indeed profound meaning beyond its immediate context (see below), but to fail to anchor it in its original setting is to run the risk of letting its interpretation drift into dangerous waters.

(b) Prediction, not static but dynamic

There is one thing, perhaps more than any other, that has brought both prophecy and apocalyptic into disrepute – the attempt to interpret ancient predictions in terms of precise contemporary or future events which are then re-interpreted when their non-fulfilment is made plain. History is replete with illustrations of this kind of prediction in which use is made of numerology, diagrams and charts, reducing inspired prophecy, by mechanical manipulation and pseudo-scientific jargon, to the level of fortune-telling.[7] Prominent in such a pursuit are the books of Ezekiel, Daniel and Revelation. The practice, of course, is as old as the apocalyptic books themselves and is commonplace in our modern world. Precise details and dates concerning the rise and fall of empires and rulers are given on the strength of ancient, esoteric tradition; the 'signs of the times' indicate that Armageddon, the war to end all wars, is near at hand; the world itself is about to come to an end.

To treat prophecy or apocalyptic in this way is, I believe, a complete misuse of scripture, using it as a wire to pick the lock of the future or finding in it some kind of secret code which, if only it can be broken, will show in precise detail the mysteries of the time to come. The consequence of such action is not only regrettable; it can at the same time be highly dangerous. A dangerous situation is created when, as has been confidently reported,[8] influential politicians and prominent military men consult Ezekiel, Daniel and Revelation as if they were some kind of horoscope and, by speculation and calculation, arrive at the conclusion that this modern nation and that modern state are to be identified as the Antichrist and the enemy of God, and that they can justifiably be destroyed by nuclear explosion in fulfilment of the will of God! The danger of such prophecy being self-fulfilling is only too apparent and carries with it a threat to the safety and survival of the whole human race.

Prophecy, it has been said, is forth-telling, not fore-telling. There is a good measure of truth in such a statement for, as E.W. Heaton says of the prophecies of Daniel, 'the writer was interested not in the mysterious future as such, but in the unveiling of the *present* sovereignty of God'.[9] And yet, that claim is only half true, for prophecy (and not least that of an apocalyptic kind) does contain a predictive element. But some words of A.M. Ramsey are of no small importance in this regard: 'It was not so much in the foreseeing of the details of events that the predictive elements lay as in the proclaiming of the divine rule over future history.'[10] These words sum up the situation to a nicety. I have elsewhere tried to express my own position in these words with reference to the interpretation of the Book of Daniel:

> It takes seriously the book's historical roots, recognizing that it was indeed 'a tract for the times' in which it was written. It takes seriously too its future reference, recognizing that prophecy finds fulfilment, not in one particular age only, but in the ongoing purpose of God . . . (Such prophecies) declare not a predetermined programme which is to work itself out inexorably and with exact precision in terms of contemporary event, but rather a divine principle which sees God in control of events rather than events in control of God.[11]

In this sense, then, it is true to say that prophecy is predictive, revealing as it does profound spiritual principles which are true for every generation, a dynamic force in today's world and not just a static force for the day in which it was first uttered.

(c) The test of scripture

The apocalyptic writers, canonical and non-canonical alike, claim to have received revelations from God by means of which the 'divine mysteries' are made known. There are times, however, when such revelations seem to owe as much to human speculation as they do to divine inspiration. Is there any reliable objective standard by which such revelations and speculations can be judged? How are we to separate the one from the other? How are we to distinguish the gold from the dross? I suggest that, to avoid the dangers of both subjective judgment and speculative prediction, the findings of the apocalyptists should be brought before the bar of scripture, and in particular New Testament scripture, and of the testimony of Jesus himself who, in transforming the hopes of the apocalyptic visionaries, fulfilled their dreams as he did those of the prophets before them. That fulfilment was in many ways quite different from the apocalyptic expectations of their day; but it penetrated to the heart of their message and gave it a meaning it otherwise would never have had. That message and that meaning, are the subject to which, in brief, we now turn.

3. THE MESSAGE OF APOCALYPTIC

It has already been pointed out in the Introduction that there is much in apocalyptic that is alien to our modern way of thinking, a fact which the succeeding chapters have helped to underline. At the same time it has been argued that, for all their differences, there is a close affinity between them which makes the message of the apocalyptic literature not altogether irrelevant to the days in which we are now living or indeed to this or any other generation. It is a message which, for all its strange and often bizarre presentation, portrays certain spiritual principles which are as true now as they were then. In outlining that message I confine myself to two simple pronouncements: the whole of history is in God's control, and the goal of history is the Kingdom of God.

(a) God is in control

In their visionary experiences and the like the apocalyptists were able, as we have seen, to bridge the gulf between heaven and earth and to see more clearly than most in their generation that what was seen was temporal and what was unseen was eternal (cf. II Cor. 4.18), and that the God whose glory filled the heavens was equally concerned about his people and about the world he had made and would bring about their salvation.

They have been described as pessimists, and that is true in so far as there was nothing they themselves could do to bring about their own deliverance. And yet at heart they were men of faith who firmly believed, despite all signs to the contrary, that God was indeed in control. Tyrants might rule, but only by the permissive will of God. Their rise and fall were known beforehand and had been predetermined by him. But in this they could plead no excuse, for each one was at the same time accountable for the evil he had done and would be brought to judgment.

That judgment too was predetermined – not just the judgment of empires and their rulers, but of individuals and angels as well. The imagery and the language may at times seem both crude and even cruel, but the message is clear enough – 'the mills of God grind slowly, but they grind exceeding small'. There is a moral factor at work in history and a judgment upon history that is inevitable and decisive. It is a judgment that falls on individuals and institutions alike as inevitably and as decisively as night follows day. There is in this literature a message of hope for the oppressed; there is also a message of judgment for the oppressor. 'They expose the unreality of all earthly power, the vanity of all worldly projects,' writes P.D. Hanson. 'They place the oppressor face to face with the ultimate Power who is their Judge and to whom they must account for their action . . . Evil will not prevail in the end. To believe otherwise would be to submit to the kind of fatalism that completely undermines the hope and courage that has characterized the lives of the saints throughout our religious history.'[12]

The fact of evil is a prevailing topic of interest and concern throughout these books. Two sources, we recall, are to be identified: the evil inclination or evil root in the human heart, and evil cosmic forces in the shape of Satan and the powers of darkness under his command. In the Day of Judgment both will be dealt with: sinners will be punished and the evil cosmic powers will be destroyed. In the New Testament also both these emphases are to be found, corresponding to what we have called the forensic and the cosmological portrayals of judgment. Sin, which is stored in the hard and impenitent heart (Rom. 2.5) will be dealt with once and for all on the Day of Judgment, and demonic powers will be put to flight.

Paul took seriously the demonic nature of evil; but it is to be observed that he no longer thought of 'principalities and powers' in terms of archons who govern the planets and stars, but rather as the sum of all those forces in the universe opposed to Christ and his church. His balanced judgment in this regard between the forensic and the cosmological, between the sinful heart within and the evil powers without, warns us against two mistakes it is very easy to make. One is the mistake of imagining that evil is to be explained simply in terms of my own wilful act of sinning. 'Evil,' says H.H. Rowley, 'is not confined to living individuals or even to a large number of individuals together, but continues from generation to generation and adheres in the totality of the whole.' Such a concept, he suggests, gives meaning to Beliar, the prince of demons who is 'the incarnate evil of the whole in each, functioning through individuals, who are also knit together in a deep unity. Beliar in other words is a reminder of the sociality of evil', to be found in societies, organizations and institutions at enmity with God.[13] The second mistake is to blame Satan and to excuse ourselves. There may be many ameliorating circumstances, but in the end we are accountable for our wilful wrongdoing; and such wrongdoing, be it in the human heart or in society at large, must come under the judgment of God. The apocalyptists would have agreed with the Mishnah tractate *Pirke 'Aboth*: 'All is foreseen, but freedom of choice is given.'

The apocalyptists, it is true, looked beyond history for the fulfilment of the divine purpose; but for them history was still the arena of God's activity on behalf of his people. In this present age evil still prevailed and oppression was still commonplace; but the ultimate power lay in the hands of God and he would in the end prevail.

(b) The Kingdom will come

Throughout this book, in describing the faith and hope of the apocalyptists, frequent use has been made of the expressions 'in the end' and 'ultimately'. These apocalyptic visionaries were able to see the hand of God in the events of their time because they were men of vision who, by divine revelation, had been shown clearly what was yet to be. They were able to interpret the happenings of history in the light of eternity. They saw meaning and judgment in history because at the end of the process lay the goal, foreordained and predetermined by God, in whose light the whole of history would at last make sense. The real significance of history for them lay in its end, its completion, its fulfilment in the coming Kingdom.

And it was this same truth that the early church was quick to grasp and to make its own. They too looked forward eagerly to the coming of the *eschatan*, the 'end', when all would be made plain. But that 'end', they believed, had in a real sense already come in Jesus and was to be made evident in the ongoing life of his church. They were to go on living out the life of the Kingdom in the here and now in the certain hope that his victory would be proclaimed when the Kingdom would come 'with power' (Cf. Mark 9.1; Rom. 1.4). In the words of Jacques Ellul, '(This) present-Kingdom is an actualizing of the *eschaton*', a realization in daily life at this present time of the presence of the end.[14] Thus, John on the isle of Patmos prays for the coming of the Kingdom with the return of his Lord: 'Even so, come, Lord Jesus!' (Rev. 22.20). But as he does so he knows that that future rule has in fact already begun: 'We give thanks to thee, Lord God Almighty, who art and who wast, that thou hast taken thy great power and begun to reign' (Rev. 11.17). To see things both as they are and as they will be, we have to begin at the end.

This 'remembrance of the future', as a key to our understanding of both past and present, is a valuable insight. As we observed in the Introduction, Wolfhart Pannenberg, for example, recognizes that, whilst history is the arena of divine revelation, it is only when viewed from the end of history that it can be seen for what it truly is. Likewise Jürgen Moltmann finds meaning and purpose in the present when it is seen in the light of a hope that is transcendent; it is a hope that is an eschatological force already at work in this present time. 'In this hope,' says Paul, 'we are saved. Now hope that is seen is not hope. For who hopes for what he sees? But if we hope for what we do not see, we wait for it with patience' (Rom 8.24f.). The coming Kingdom, which is the focus of this hope, contains within itself a power that penetrates the present and becomes an effective force in the here and now. It gives the assurance of victory long before the conflict is over and even in face of apparent defeat.

The apocalyptists looked to the Kingdom as a future event; but it is of interest to note that, among the Qumran Community at any rate, 'eternal life' which was a mark of the Kingdom was something they possessed even now at this present time. We are reminded of the teaching of Jesus in this regard for whom the Kingdom was both present and to come. It is 'the Kingdom on earth' and it is 'the Kingdom in heaven'. It is not an either-or; it is a both-and. It is future and other-worldly in the sense that it speaks, not of our breaking through to God, but of his breaking through to us; not of human programmes achieving success, but of divine purpose expressing wholeness; not of human striving after perfection, but of divine action effecting salvation. And it is this-worldly and present in the sense that the earth is the stage on which we are to see the divine enactment of the scenario of salvation.

The message of the Kingdom presents us with an integrated world-view in which there is a close correspondence between earth and heaven, between the events of 'this world' and the events of 'that other world'. The reality that is portrayed here is but part of the reality that is portrayed there. Together they make up that one world that alone makes sense of the tragedies and injustices of human life and human history. It is this total reality that alone can display that coherent pattern which expresses the divine purpose. To see the 'visible earthly pattern' as a thing by itself is to see only half the picture. To see it whole is to view life from God's perspective.

The time will come when the 'wholeness' of God's world will at last be revealed, when we shall 'understand even as also we are understood' (I Cor. 13.12). There are eternal realities beyond the sense of either sight or touch. But gullibly we accept the tangible as the real, the transient as the eternal. The two 'worlds' are in fact to be seen together, for only then do the events of human life fall into place. No single part of it is unredeemable. Even the natural tragedies, the cruelties of 'blind fate', the chance happenings that bring total disaster will be seen to have meaning after all. This is certainly the conviction of the apostle Paul: constrained by the love of Christ (II Cor. 5.14) we begin to see that evil, tragedy and loss are not simply defeated or nullified or neutralized; they are redeemed, so that, in the providence of God, good comes out of evil and gain comes out of loss.

This leads on to one final reflection: the coming of the Kingdom means consummation. The End will be a new Beginning in which all things, even the earth itself, will share. In the apocalyptic books this great event is described in many varied ways, but remains a 'mystery'. In the New Testament the key to that mystery is to be found in the *parousia* of the Lord himself, the Messiah who is the heavenly Son of Man. The manner of his appearing in glory, like the manner of his coming to Bethlehem, is concealed in the mystery of God's eternal purpose for the world and its redemption. Within the New Testament, and in particular in the Book of Revelation, that appearing is described in the idiom of apocalyptic and in the thought-form of that day. We may try to demythologize and transfer its symbols into present-day idiom, but the fact itself is surely founded on the revelation of scripture and on the conviction of Jesus himself. The church's cry continues to be *maranatha*, and its prayer 'Thy Kingdom come . . . on earth as it is in heaven.'

Notes

Notes

Introduction

1. R.H. Charles (ed.), *The Apocrypha and Pseudepigrapha of the Old Testament*, vols 1 and 2, Clarendon Press 1913.
2. H.H. Rowley, *The Relevance of Apocalyptic*, Lutterworth Press 1944; 3rd edn 1963.
3. E.W. Nicholson, 'Apocalyptic', *Tradition and Interpretation, Essays by members of the Society for Old Testament Study* ed. G.W. Anderson, Clarendon Press 1979, p.189.
4. James H. Charlesworth (ed.), *The Old Testament Pseudepigrapha*, vols 1 and 2, Darton, Longman and Todd 1983 and 1985.
5. H.F.D. Sparks (ed.), *The Apocryphal Old Testament*, Clarendon Press 1984.
6. G.F. Moore, *Judaism in the First Century of the Christian Era*, vols 1–3, Harvard University Press 1932.
7. R.T. Herford, *Talmud and Apocrypha*, Soncino Press 1933.
8. K. Koch, *The Rediscovery of Apocalyptic*, SCM Press 1972.
9. Ernst Käsemann, 'The Beginnings of Christian Theology', *New Testament Questions of Today*, SCM Press and Fortress Press 1969, p. 102.
10. K. Koch, op. cit., p.14.
11. Some of the ramifications of this are set out by Christopher Rowland, *The Open Heaven*, SPCK and Crossroad 1982, and *Christian Origins*, SPCK 1985. See also *Apocalyptic and the New Testament* ed. J. Marcus and M.L. Soards, JSOT Press, Sheffield 1989.
12. W. Pannenberg, 'Redemptive Event and History', *Basic Questions in Theology*, SCM Press and Fortress Press 1970, pp. 15–80.
13. Jürgen Moltmann, *Theology of Hope: On the Ground and Implications of a Christian Eschatology*, SCM Press and Harper 1967.

14. P.D. Hanson (ed.), *Visionaries and their Apocalypses*, SPCK and Fortress Press 1983, p. 8.

15. James Barr, 'Jewish Apocalyptic in Recent Scholarly Study', *Bulletin of the John Rylands Library*, 58, 1975, pp. 9–35.

16. P.D. Hanson, op. cit., p. 2.

17. Ibid., p. 8.

18. D.S. Russell, *Apocalyptic: Ancient and Modern*, SCM Press and Fortress Press 1978, p.8.

I *The Literature: Identification and Definition*

1. See further pp. 14–19.

2. D.S. Russell, *The Old Testament Pseudepigrapha: Patriarchs and Prophets in Early Judaism*, SCM Press and Fortress Press 1987, pp. xiif.

3. See R.H. Charles, op. cit.; James H. Charlesworth, op. cit.; H.F.D. Sparks, op. cit.; D.S. Russell, op. cit.

4. Matthew Black, *The Scrolls and Christian Origins*, Thomas Nelson and Sons 1961, p. 8.

5. See J.T. Milik, *Ten Years of Discovery in the Wilderness of Judaea*, SCM Press 1959, pp. 32ff.

6. For a list of these works see D.S. Russell, *The Method and Message of Jewish Apocalyptic*, SCM Press and Westminster Press 1964, pp. 38–48.

7. J.J. Collins, 'Was the Dead Sea Sect an Apocalyptic Movement?', *Archaeology and History in the Dead Sea Scrolls* ed. Lawrence H. Schiffman, *Journal for the Study of the Pseudepigrapha, Supplement Series 8*, JSOT/ASOR Monographs 2, Sheffield 1990, pp. 44f.

8. D.S. Russell, *Apocalyptic: Ancient and Modern*, p. 1.

9. H.H. Rowley, *The Relevance of Apocalyptic*, 1963, pp. 148f.

10. Cf. J.J. Collins, *Daniel, with an Introduction to Apocalyptic Literature*, William B. Eerdmans 1984, pp. 2–3.

11. J. Lindblom, *Die Jesaja-Apokalypse*, Lund 1938, pp. 101f.

12. D.S. Russell, *The Method and Message of Jewish Apocalyptic*, pp. 104ff.

13. Klaus Koch, *The Rediscovery of Apocalyptic*, pp. 18ff.

14. Ibid., pp. 23–33.

15. P.D. Hanson, 'Jewish Apocalyptic against its Near Eastern Environment', *Revue Biblique*, lxxviii, 1971, pp. 31–58; 'Old Testament Apocalyptic Re-examined', *Interpretation* 25, 1971, pp. 454–479 (included as ch. 3 in P.D. Hanson (ed.), *Visionaries and their Apocalypses*); *The Dawn of Apocalyptic*, Fortress Press 1975.

16. P.D. Hanson, *The Dawn of Apocalyptic*, p. 11.

17. M.A. Knibb, 'Prophecy and the emergence of the Jewish apocalypses',

Israel's Prophetic Tradition: Essays in Honour of Peter Ackroyd ed. R. Coggins, A. Phillips and M.A. Knibb, Cambridge University Press 1982.

18. M.E. Stone, 'Lists of Revealed Things in the Apocalyptic Literature', *Magnalia Dei: The Mighty Acts of God: Essays on the Bible and Archaeology in memory of G. Ernest Wright* ed. F.M. Cross, W.E. Lemke and P.D. Miller, Doubleday 1976.

19. Christopher Rowland, *The Open Heaven*, p. 14.

20. See R.E. Sturm, 'Defining the word "Apocalyptic"', *Apocalyptic and the New Testament* ed. J. Marcus and M.L. Soards, JSOT Press, Sheffield 1989.

21. See *Apocalypse: The Morphology of a Genre, Semeia 14* ed. J.J. Collins, Scholars Press 1979.

22. Ibid., p. 9.

23. See J.J. Collins, op. cit., pp. 1ff.

II Apocalyptic: Its Birth and Growth

1. André Lacocque, *Daniel in his Time*, University of South Carolina Press 1988, p. 89.

2. See D.S. Russell, *The Method and Message of Jewish Apocalyptic*, pp. 178ff.

3. P.D. Hanson, 'Jewish Apocalyptic against its Near Eastern Environment', pp. 31–58, and 'Old Testament Apocalyptic Re-examined', pp. 454–479.

4. P.D. Hanson, 'Jewish Apocalyptic against its Near Eastern Environment', p. 34.

5. O. Plöger, *Theocracy and Eschatology*, Blackwell and John Knox Press 1968.

6. R.E. Clements, 'The Interpretation of Prophecy and the Origin of Apocalyptic', *Bible, Church and World* ed. J.H.Y. Briggs, Baptist Union Press 1989, pp. 28ff.

7. G. von Rad, *Old Testament Theology*, vol. 2, Harper and Row and Oliver and Boyd 1965; reissued SCM Press 1973.

8. For helpful summaries and assessments of scholarly opinion, see E.W. Nicholson, 'Apocalyptic', pp. 189–213, and M.A. Knibb, 'Prophecy and the emergence of the Jewish apocalypses'.

9. See J.Z. Smith, 'Wisdom and Apocalyptic', *Religious Syncretism in Antiquity* ed. B.A. Pearson, 1975; included as ch. 6 in P.D. Hanson, *Visionaries and their Apocalypses*, 1983.

10. See J.J. Collins, *The Apocalyptic Vision of the Book of Daniel*, Harvard Semitic Monographs 16, Scholars Press 1977, pp. 56–58.

11. J.Z. Smith, op. cit., 1983, p. 115.

12. R.P. Carroll, 'Twilight of Prophecy or Dawn of Apocalyptic?', *Journal for the Study of the Old Testament* 14, 1979, p. 29.

13. P.D. Hanson, 'Old Testament Apocalyptic Re-examined', *Visionaries and their Apocalypses*, p. 53.

14. See D.S. Russell, *The Method and Message of Jewish Apocalyptic*, pp. 173–175.

15. P.R. Ackroyd, *Israel under Babylon and Persia*, Clarendon Press 1970, p. 344.

16. See Margaret Barker, *The Older Testament: the Survival of Themes from the Ancient Royal Cult in Sectarian Judaism and Early Christianity*, SPCK 1987.

17. O. Plöger, op. cit.

18. See E.W. Nicholson, art. cit., pp. 202ff.

19. P.D. Hanson, 'Old Testament Apocalyptic Re-examined'.

20. Ibid., p. 49.

21. Ibid., p. 23.

22. Ibid., p. 48.

23. Ibid., p. 49.

24. R.P. Carroll, art. cit.

25. Ibid., p. 18.

26. André Lacocque, op. cit., p. 91.

27. M.A. Knibb, art. cit.

28. Ibid., p. 176.

29. E.W. Heaton, *The Book of Daniel*, SCM Press 1956, p. 18.

III Apocalyptic Groups and Apocalyptic Books

1. See Margaret Barker, *The Lost Prophet*, SPCK 1988, pp. 8ff.

2. For a fuller summary of the contents of I Enoch and other apocalyptic books, see G.W.E. Nickelsburg, *Jewish Literature between the Bible and the Mishnah*, SCM Press and Fortress Press 1981, and D.S. Russell, *The Old Testament Pseudepigrapha: Patriarchs and Prophets in Early Judaism*. For texts and introductions see James H. Charlesworth (ed.), *The Old Testament Pseudepigrapha*, 2 vols, and H.F.D. Sparks (ed.), *The Apocryphal Old Testament*.

3. Michael E. Stone, 'Enoch and Apocalyptic Origins', *Visionaries and their Apocalypses*, p. 94.

4. See further D.S. Russell, *The Old Testament Pseudepigrapha*, pp. 24ff.

5. See Michael E. Stone, art. cit., p. 99.

6. Cf. Margaret Barker, *The Older Testament*.

7. Cf. Carey A. Moore, *Daniel, Esther and Jeremiah: the Additions*, Anchor Bible, Doubleday 1977, pp. 5ff.

8. Cf. J.T. Milik, 'Prière de Nabonide et autres écrits d'un cycle de Daniel', *Revue Biblique*, 1956, pp. 411–415.

9. Cf. J.C. VanderKam, *Textual and Historical Studies*, Scholars Press 1977, p. 283.

10. O.S. Wintermute in James H. Charlesworth, op. cit., vol. 2, pp. 43ff.

11. F.M. Cross, *The Ancient Library of Qumran and Modern Biblical Studies*, revd edn, Duckworth 1961, p. 199.

12. M. Testuz, *Les Idées Religieuses du Livre des Jubilés*, Librairie E. Droz, Geneva 1960.

13. Michael E. Stone, art. cit., p. 100.

14. This is how it is classified by James H. Charlesworth, op. cit., p. vi.

IV Revelation: Its Reception and Expression

1. See W.D. Davies, *Torah in the Messianic Age and/or the Age to Come*, SBL, Philadelphia 1952; G.F. Moore, *Judaism in the First Century of the Christian Era*, vol. 1; Jacob Neusner, *Torah through the Ages*, SCM Press and Trinity Press International 1990; E.P. Sanders, *Paul, the Law and the Jewish People*, SCM Press and Fortress Press 1985.

2. André Lacocque, *Daniel in his Time*, p. 189.

3. D.S. Russell, *The Method and Message of Jewish Apocalyptic*, p. 118.

4. Ibid., pp. 127–140.

5. See J.W. Rogerson, 'The Hebrew Conception of Corporate Personality: a Re-examination', *Journal of Theological Studies* 21; and J. Barr, *The Semantics of Biblical Language*, Oxford University Press 1961; reissued SCM Press 1983, pp. 8ff.

6. J.J. Collins, *The Apocalyptic Vision of the Book of Daniel*, p. 72.

7. A.R.C. Leaney, *The Rule of Qumran and its Meaning*, SCM Press 1966, pp. 67f.

8. Thomas J. Sappington, *Revelation and Redemption at Colossae*, JSOT Press 1991, pp. 78ff.

9. Cf. S. Niditch, 'The Visionary', *Ideal Figures in Ancient Judaism* ed. J.J. Collins and G.W.E. Nickelsburg, Scholars Press 1980, pp. 153–179.

V Divine Secrets Revealed

1. See M.E. Stone, 'Lists of Revealed Things', *Magnalia Dei: The Mighty Acts of God* ed. F.M. Cross *et al.*, Doubleday 1975, pp. 414–52; Christopher Rowland, *The Open Heaven*, pp. 73–191.

2. D.S. Russell, *The Method and Message of Jewish Apocalyptic*, pp. 205–234.

3. Christopher Rowland, op. cit., pp. 143f.

4. André Lacocque, op. cit., p. 89.

5. S. Mowinckel, *He that Cometh*, Blackwell 1959, p. 271.

6. J.J. Collins, 'Apocalyptic Eschatology and the Transcendence of Death', *Visionaries and their Apocalypses*, p. 68.

7. Ibid., p. 68. Such insights warn us, as Collins indicates, not to contrast too sharply Greek thought and Hebrew thought in this connection as has often been done (not least by me!). There are clear affinities between, on the one hand, the apocalyptic hope which draws on the Old Testament tradition of the Heavenly Council (cf. Job 1.6ff.; Isa. 6.6ff.; Pss. 82.1; 89.7) and, on the other hand, the Platonic tradition with its 'world of ideas' and its hope of the immortality of the soul.

8. Ibid., pp. 72f.

9. Christopher Rowland, op. cit., p. 188.

VI Dualism and Apocalyptic

1. For a helpful outline of this subject see Benedikt Otzen, *Judaism in Antiquity*, JSOT Press 1990, pp. 84–92, 171–218; and Martinus C. de Boer, 'Paul and Jewish Apocalyptic Eschatology', in Joel Marcus and Marion L. Soards (eds), *Apocalyptic and the New Testament*, pp. 169–191.

2. André Lacocque, *Daniel in his Time*, pp. 105f.

3. Benedikt Otzen, p. 90.

VII Messiah and 'Son of Man'

1. For a fuller treatment see D.S. Russell, *The Method and Message of Jewish Apocalyptic*, ch. 12; and *The Old Testament Pseudepigrapha*, pp. 123–128.

2. James D.G. Dunn, *Christology in the Making*, SCM Press and Westminster Press 1984; 2nd edn 1989, pp. 84, 93.

3. G.F. Moore, *Judaism*, vol. 2, *Harvard University Press* 1932, p. 244.

4. Geza Vermes, *Jesus the Jew*, Collins 1973; 2nd edn SCM Press and Fortress Press 1983, p. 138.

5. D.S. Russell, *The Method and Message of Jewish Apocalyptic*, pp. 324ff.

6. Geza Vermes, op. cit., p. 168.

7. Christopher Rowland, *The Open Heaven*, pp. 178ff.

8. See André Lacocque, *The Book of Daniel*.

9. Translation by Geza Vermes, *The Dead Sea Scrolls in English*, Penguin Books 1962; 3rd edn 1987.

10. E.W. Heaton, *The Book of Daniel*, p. 184.

11. Cf. Christopher Rowland, op. cit., pp. 186f.

12. J.T. Milik, *Ten Years of Discovery in the Wilderness of Judaea*, p. 33.

13. Geza Vermes, op. cit., p. 176.

14. E.g. R.H. Charles (first century BC), E. Sjöberg (beginning of the Christian era), M. Casey (between 100 BC and AD 70).

15. Geza Vermes, op. cit., p. 175.

16. Matthew Black, 'A Bibliography on I Enoch in the Eighties', *Journal for the Study of the Pseudepigrapha* Issue 5, Sheffield Academic Press 1989, p. 9.

17. Ibid., p. 8.

18. James D.G. Dunn, op. cit., p. 87.

VIII *Apocalyptic Interpretation: A Christian Perspective*

1. Christopher Rowland, *The Open Heaven*, p. 358.

2. See Klaus Koch, *The Rediscovery of Apocalyptic*.

3. For examples of such influence see the essays in honour of J. Louis Martyn in *Apocalyptic and the New Testament* ed. Joel Marcus and Marion L. Soards.

4. G. Ebeling, 'The Beginning of Christian Theology', *Apocalypticism* ed. R.W. Funk, *Journal for Theology and the Church* 6, 1969, p. 58.

5. E.F. Scott, *The Kingdom and the Messiah*, T. and T. Clark 1911, p. 91, quoted by H.H. Rowley, *The Relevance of Apocalyptic*, p. 192 n. 1.

6. Eg. *There's a New World Coming*, Bantam 1984; *The Late Great Planet Earth* (with C.C. Carlson), Bantam 1983, Zondervan 1988, and *Satan is Alive and Well on Planet Earth* (with C.C. Carlson), Zondervan 1989.

7. For examples see Paul D. Hanson, *Old Testament Apocalyptic*, Abingdon Press 1987, pp. 44ff.

8. For documented evidence see Grace Halsell, *Prophecy and Politics: Militant Evangelists on the Road to Nuclear War*, Lawrence Hill and Co., Westport 1986.

9. E.W. Heaton, *The Book of Daniel*, p. 37.

10. A.M. Ramsey, 'The Authority of the Bible', *Peak's Commentary on the Bible* (revised edition) ed. Matthew Black and H.H. Rowley, Thomas Nelson and Sons 1962, p. 2 section 2d.

11. D.S. Russell, *Daniel: an Active Volcano*, St Andrew Press and Westminster/John Knox Press 1989, p. 15.

12. P.D. Hanson, *Old Testament Apocalyptic*, pp. 63f.

13. H.H. Rowley, op. cit., pp. 177f.

14. Jacques Ellul, *The Presence of the Kingdom*, SCM Press 1957, p. 56.

A Select Bibliography

James Barr, 'Jewish Apocalyptic in Recent Scholarly Study', in *Bulletin of the John Rylands Library* 58, 1975–6, pp. 9–35.

R.P. Carroll, 'Twilight of Prophecy or Dawn of Apocalyptic?', *Journal for the Study of the Old Testament* 14, 1979, pp. 3–35.

J.H. Charlesworth (ed.), *The Old Testament Pseudepigrapha*, vol. 1, Darton, Longman and Todd 1983.

J.J. Collins, *The Apocalyptic Vision of the Book of Daniel*, Harvard Semitic Monographs 16, Scholars Press 1977.

—— *Apocalypse: the Morphology of a Genre* (ed.), Semeia 14, Scholars Press 1979.

—— 'Apocalyptic Eschatology as the Transcendence of Death', *Catholic Biblical Quarterly* 36, 1974, pp. 21–43; included as ch. 3 in *Visionaries and their Apocalypses* ed. P.D. Hanson, SPCK and Fortress Press, Philadelphia 1983.

—— *Daniel, with an Introduction to Apocalyptic Literature*, William B. Eerdmans, Grand Rapids 1984.

—— 'Apocalyptic Literature', *Early Judaism and its Modern Interpreters* ed. R.A. Kraft and G.W.E. Nickelsburg, Fortress Press and Scholars Press 1986.

P.D. Hanson, *The Dawn of Apocalyptic*, Fortress Press 1975.

—— 'Apocalypse, Genre' and 'Apocalypticism', *Interpreter's Dictionary of the Bible*, Suppl. Vol., Abingdon Press, Nashville 1976, pp. 27–34.

—— *Visionaries and their Apocalypses* (ed.), SPCK and Fortress Press 1983.

—— *Old Testament Apocalyptic*, Abingdon Press 1987.

D. Hellholm (ed.), *Apocalypticism in the Mediterranean World*, Mohr-Siebeck, Tübingen 1983.

M.A. Knibb, 'Prophecy and the emergence of the Jewish apocalypses', *Israel's*

Prophetic Tradition: Essays in Honour of Peter Ackroyd ed. R. Coggins, A. Phillips and M.A. Knibb, Cambridge University Press 1982.

K. Koch, *The Rediscovery of Apocalyptic*, SCM Press 1972; ch. 3 included as ch. 1 in P.D. Hanson (ed.), *Visionaries and their Apocalypses*, SPCK and Fortress Press 1983.

André Lacocque, *Daniel in his Time*, University of South Carolina Press 1988.

E.W. Nicholson, 'Apocalyptic', *Tradition and Interpretation, Essays by members of the Society for Old Testament Study* ed. G.W. Anderson, Clarendon Press 1979, pp. 189–213.

Benedikt Otzen, *Judaism in Antiquity*, JSOT Press, Sheffield 1990, ch. 5.

O. Plöger, *Theocracy and Eschatology*, John Knox Press and Blackwell 1968.

M. Rist, 'Apocalypticism', *Interpreter's Dictionary of the Bible*, vol. 1, Abingdon Press 1962, pp. 157ff.

Christopher Rowland, *The Open Heaven*, SPCK and Crossroad, New York 1982.

H.H. Rowley, *The Relevance of Apocalyptic*, 3rd edn Lutterworth Press, 1963.

D.S. Russell, *The Method and Message of Jewish Apocalyptic*, SCM Press and Westminster Press, Philadelphia 1964.

—— *Apocalyptic: Ancient and Modern*, SCM Press and Fortress Press 1978.

T.J. Sappington, *Revelation and Redemption at Colossae*, JSNT Supplement Series 53, JSOT Press, Sheffield 1991.

H.F.D. Sparks (ed.), *The Apocryphal Old Testament*, Clarendon Press 1984.

M.E. Stone, 'Lists of Revealed Things in the Apocalyptic Literature', *Magnalia Dei: The Mighty Acts of God: Essays on the Bible and Archaeology in memory of G. Ernest Wright* ed. F.M. Cross, W.E. Lemke and P.D. Miller, Doubleday, New York 1976, pp. 414–452.

Geza Vermes, *The Dead Sea Scrolls in English*, Penguin Books, 3rd edn 1987.

P. Vielhauer, 'Apocalyptic in Early Christianity' in E. Hennecke, *New Testament Apocrypha* vol. 2 ed. W. Schneemelcher, Lutterworth Press and Westminster Press, Philadelphia 1965; reissued SCM Press 1974, pp. 608–683.

Indexes

Index of Texts

INDEX OF TEXTS

III The Pseudepigrapha

Index of Authors

INDEX OF AUTHORS

Index of Subjects

INDEX OF SUBJECTS

Qumran, xv, 5, 6, 35, 36, 37, 45, 48,
  53, 82, 84, 92, 93, 98, 107, 114,
  117, 118, 122, 126, 138
  and apocalyptic literature, xv, 5, 6,
    35, 45, 53, 113
  and Essenses, 4
  and priests, 23f.
  and literature, 4f., 48
  milieu of, 8

Raphael, 111
Raz, 82
Resurrection, 40, 57, 97, 100f., 102,
  120
  body, 58, 70, 100, 101f.
  in Daniel, 96, 97, 100f., 102
  in Isaiah Apocalypse, 96
  participants in, 100f.
Revelation, 5, 39, 47, 49, 54, 55, 67,
  75, 78, 79, 91, 105, 129, 130
  and inspiration, 30, 60ff.
  and pseudonymity, 65
  and Torah, 60f., 62
  and wisdom, 61
  media of, 71ff.
  methods of, 65ff.
  objective, 73
  of hidden things, 4, 11, 42, 69, 71,
    83, 134

Satan, 50, 52, 104, 110f., 114, 115, 129,
  136
Scribalism, 21ff., 31
Scribe
  as Enoch, 37, 41, 125
  as Ezra, 60
  ideal, 31
Scripture, 80, 129ff., 133, 134f.
Secret(s) (see Mysteries), 31, 33, 39, 41,
  42, 62, 68, 69, 71, 77, 82ff., 89,
  106, 108, 129, 133
  books, 77, 78ff., 82, 130
  in Daniel, 82
  in heaven, 82, 83, 105
  in Qumran, 82
  lists of, 83
  oaths, 85
  of creation, 22, 84
  tradition, 62, 90
Semjaza, 110
Seventy, 63, 71

books, 57, 63
years, 47, 80, 90
Shamanism, 64, 74, 75
Sheol, 39, 98, 100
  compartments in, 99, 101
  intermediate state, 100
  place of judgment, 100
Son of man, 37, 39, 42, 121ff.
  and Jesus, 124, 126f.
  as angel, 122
  as Enoch, 125, 126
  as Messiah, 103, 121ff., 123f., 125,
    126, 139
  as Michael, 122, 126
  as title, 121, 124, 125
  in Daniel, 120, 121, 123
  in IV Ezra, 123f.
  in Similitudes of Enoch, 95, 124f.
Speculation, xviii, 37, 40f., 41, 42, 43,
  51, 66, 82, 84, 86, 103, 106, 116,
  118, 124, 130, 131, 134
Spirit
  of truth and error, 114f.
Stars, 55, 70, 84
  as angels, 40, 54, 70, 97, 111
Suffering Servant, 39, 131
Swd, 63, 82
Symbol(ism), xix, 40, 57, 63, 70f., 72,
  76, 118, 120, 122, 124

Taurus, 84
Temple, 25, 43, 60, 61, 70, 94
  centrality of, 23
  cult of, 28, 42
  destruction of, 17, 28, 51
  heavenly, 41
  rededication of, 18
  restoration of, 26, 55
Theodicy, 51, 57, 59, 104
Throne of God (see *Merkabah*), 10, 25,
  26, 39, 53, 54, 55, 76, 84ff., 103
Torah (see Law), 112, 114
  and apocalyptic, 61ff.
  and revelation, 61
  oral, 33, 61, 65
  written, 61
Two ages, 9, 92, 107ff., 129
Two dimensions, 106f.
Two spirits, 114f.
Two ways, 111ff.
Two worlds, 105f.

163